FRIEDRICH KIESLER: ENDLESS HOUSE

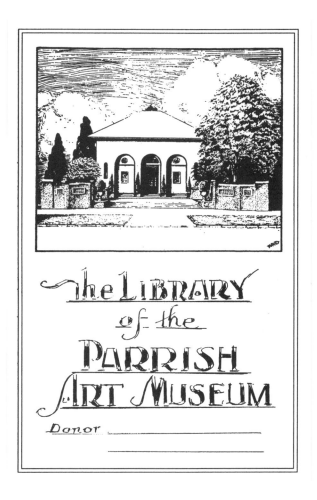

Architecture without Poetry is nothing but a protective umbrella (of straw, skin or stone) against unfavorable climatic conditions – and against attacks from human and other animals during sleep.

Frederick Kiesler, *Magic Architecture*, typescript, 1940s

Architektur ohne Poesie ist weiter nichts als ein Schutzschild (aus Stroh, Haut oder Stein) gegen widrige Witterungseinflüsse – und gegen Angriffe von menschlichen und anderen Tieren, während man schläft.

Friedrich Kiesler, *Magic Architecture*, Typoskript, 40er-Jahre

HATJE CANTZ

FRIEDRICH KIESLER–ZENTRUM, WIEN **FRIEDRICH KIESLER: ENDLESS HOUSE**

MMK – MUSEUM FÜR MODERNE KUNST FRANKFURT AM MAIN

1   FREDERICK KIESLER WITH *ENDLESS HOUSE* MODEL
    IN PROGRESS, AROUND 1959
    **FRIEDRICH KIESLER BEI DER ARBEIT AM MODELL
    DES *ENDLESS HOUSE* , UM 1959**

(56). Page 303

Project for a Space-House. (insert)
Model built 1933 in New York. An attempt to break up the whol
house-area into many rooms of different sizes (if necessary) o
to combine several rooms into one or two large areas.
(From the Archit. Record)(Kiesler, New York)

Photo taken at the International Exhibition, New York 1926.
Shows scale model of the "Endless" and is the
background reliefs by Picasso,
part of another Exhibit—

"...of the hemisphere, which are infinite
and divided by an infinite number

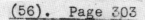

Spheroid model of the
"Endless House"

"Space—House"

Paris
1924
New York
34

both of these projects were designed by Kiesler, "structures in continuous tension" to facilitate pre—and—fabrication in moulds for plastics, as well as to shelter those "continuous mutations" of the life-force, which seem to be part of the "practical" as well as of the magical.

PREFACE
VORWORT

**UDO KITTELMANN
DIETER BOGNER**

An important strategy in the programme of Frankfurt's Museum of Modern Art (MMK) is to host archives by other institutions, such as the archive of the Frederick Kiesler Center. This idea is compatible with the goals of the Kiesler Center in Vienna. The museum aims to show a different archive each year, in order that the complex contents and materials inside these »treasuries of knowledge and memory« – usually available to scholars only – are made accessible to the public. The Kiesler Center is particularly interested in connecting the holistic, architectural and artistic concepts of the visionary Austro-American Frederick Kiesler (1890–1965) to contemporary art. Kiesler's ideas are today more up-to-date than ever.

Kiesler's exhibition design for Peggy Guggenheim's gallery *Art of This Century* (New York, 1942) was the first of three presentations during the eighteen months of the Kiesler Center at the MMK. A catalogue was also published on this occasion. This second presentation focuses on one of the 20th Century architectural icons, the *Endless House*, a visionary project Kiesler worked on from the 1940s until his death in 1965. This »total« house remained unrealized, however, the history of its influence is »endless«, reaching its zenith in the present times.

The exhibition at the MMK provides a multi-layered insight into the *Endless House*'s development from the early stages up to the larger architectural plans drawn up for his client Mary Sisler in the 1960s. An extensive selection of sketches and plans, photographs of both the unfinished and completed models, theoretical texts as well as letters, publications and newspaper reports offer a comprehensive overview of Kiesler's complex way of thinking and its formal expression.

The interactive exhibition architecture by casino.container (Detlef Meyer-Voggenreiter, Uwe Wagner and Claudia Hoffmann) has already successfully presented the archive material and also offers an ideal format for the *Endless House*.

We would like to thank everyone participating in the project, above all the exhibition curator, Harald Krejci, as well as Eva Christina Kraus for her support and Valentina Sonzogni for academic research. Our partner at the MMK, Mario Kramer, contributed to the development and the realization of the project. Special thanks to Jason McCoy for the loan of an *Endless House* model from 1959.

Presently, the next presentation on Kiesler's theory of *Correalism* is in preparation and this will complete the cooperation between the Frederick Kiesler Center and the Museum of Modern Art in Frankfurt.

Das Archiv des Friedrich Kiesler-Zentrums zu Gast im Museum für Moderne Kunst Frankfurt (MMK) ist ein wichtiger Teilaspekt der Ausstellungsstrategie des Museums und trifft sich mit dem Konzept des in Wien beheimateten Friedrich Kiesler-Zentrums. Eine der Zielsetzungen des Museums ist die jährlich wechselnde Präsentation unterschiedlichster externer Archive, um der Öffentlichkeit die komplexe Inhaltlichkeit und Materialität dieser zumeist nur Wissenschaftlern zugänglichen »Schatzkammern des Wissens und der Erinnerung« temporär zu öffnen. Das Interesse des Kiesler-Zentrums gilt der Verbindung der ganzheitlichen architektonisch-künstlerischen Konzepte des österreichisch-amerikanischen Visionärs Friedrich Kiesler (1890–1965) mit dem zeitgenössischen Kunstgeschehen. Seine Ideen sind heute aktueller denn je.

Den Auftakt der achtzehnmonatigen Präsenz des Archivs des Friedrich Kiesler-Zentrums im MMK machte die Ausstellungsgestaltung Kieslers für Peggy Guggenheims Galerie *Art of This Century* 1942 in New York, zu der ebenfalls eine Publikation erschienen ist. Die achtzehn Präsentation konzentriert sich auf eine Architektur-Ikone des 20. Jahrhunderts: Kieslers *Endless House*, eine visionäre architektonische Konzeption, an der er von den vierziger Jahren bis zu seinem Tod arbeitete. Zur Ausführung ist dieses »totale« Haus nie gekommen. Seine Wirkungsgeschichte ist jedoch »endlos« und erreicht gegenwärtig einen neuen Höhepunkt.

Die Ausstellung im MMK gewährt einen vielschichtigen Einblick in den Entwicklungsprozess des *Endless House* von der Frühphase in den vierziger Jahren bis zu den großen Architekturplänen für das *Endless House* für Mary Sisler in den sechziger Jahren. Eine umfangreiche Auswahl von Skizzen und Plänen, Modellaufnahmen und Arbeitsfotos, theoretischen Abhandlungen und Briefen, Publikationen und Zeitungsberichten bietet einen umfassenden Einblick in das komplexe inhaltliche Denken Kieslers und dessen formalen Ausdruck.

Die von casino.container (Detlef Meyer-Voggenreiter, Uwe Wagner and Claudia Hoffmann) geschaffene interaktive Ausstellungsarchitektur hat ihre Feuerprobe bereits bei der ersten Präsentation der Archivmaterialien bestanden. Sie bietet auch für das *Endless House* ideale Voraussetzungen.

Dank gilt allen an diesem Projekt Beteiligten: vor allem dem Kurator der Ausstellung, Harald Krejci, Leiter der Sammlungen des Friedrich Kiesler-Zentrums, sowie Eva Christina Kraus für ihre konzeptionelle Unterstützung und Valentina Sonzogni für wissenschaftliche Recherchen. Mario Kramer hat als verantwortlicher Partner die besten Voraussetzungen für die Projektabwicklung im MMK geschaffen. Jason McCoy stellte ein Modell des *Endless House* aus dem Jahr 1959 zur Verfügung.

Als dritte Präsentation und Abschluss der Zusammenarbeit des Friedrich Kiesler-Zentrums mit dem Museum für Moderne Kunst Frankfurt ist eine Präsentation zu Kieslers Theorie des *Correalismus* in Vorbereitung.

4 KIESLER WITH THE MODEL OF THE *ENDLESS HOUSE*,
AROUND 1960
KIESLER MIT DEM MODELL DES *ENDLESS HOUSE*,
UM 1960

HARALD KREJCI

ZUM KONZEPT DES ENDLESS HOUSE 1947-1961

1   The »Manifeste du Corréa-
    lisme« was first published in: *Archi-
    tecture d'Aujourdhui*, Paris
    1949.

1   Das »Manifeste du Corréa-
    lisme« erscheint erstmals in:
    Architecture d'Aujourd'hui,
    Paris 1949.

2   See Kiesler's paper on
    »Pseudofunctionalism and
    Modern Architecture«, as well
    as selected publications by
    Kiesler referred to in the
    annex.

2   Siehe dazu den Text Kieslers
    »Pseudofunctionalism and
    Modern Architecture« sowie
    die ausgewählte Bibliografie zu
    Kieslers Schriften im Anhang.

3   Thus, Kiesler does not feature
    in relevant publications on
    utopian architecture, such as
    Heinrich Klotz's *Visionäre
    Architektur* (1986) or in Niko-
    laus Pevsner's *Architek-
    turgeschichte* (1966). Hanno-
    Walter Kruft dedicates a mere
    footnote to Kiesler in his
    *Geschichte der Architekturtheo-
    rie* (1985). It is thanks to Dieter
    Bogner, amongst others, that
    Kiesler's work eventually
    gained recognition. See rele-
    vant literature referred to in
    the annex.

3   So scheint Kiesler in ein-
    schlägigen Publikationen zur
    utopischen Architektur, wie
    etwa in Heinrich Klotz' *Vision
    der Moderne* (1986) oder in
    Nikolaus Pevsners *Lexikon der
    Weltarchitektur* (1966) nicht
    auf. Hanno-Walter Kruft gönnt
    Kiesler in seiner *Geschichte der
    Architekturtheorie* (1985) nur
    eine Fußnote. Es kommt u. a.
    Dieter Bogner der Verdienst
    zu, die Rezeption von Kieslers
    Werk eingeleitet zu haben.
    Siehe hierzu die Bibliografie im
    Anhang.

4   See Friedrich Kiesler
    »Pseudofunctionalism and
    Modern Architecture«, in:
    Partisan Review, July 1949,
    as printed in the catalogue

4   Siehe die im Katalog abge-
    druckte Version von Friedrich
    Kieslers »Pseudofunctionalism
    and Modern Architecture«, in:
    Partisan Review, Juli 1949

By the time Frederick Kiesler presented his architectural model of an *Endless House* to the *Visionary Architecture* Exhibition at the Museum of Modern Art in New York in 1960, he had already spent fifteen years on this complex of ideas. Kiesler's work on the *Endless House*, a single family dwelling that was never built, is built upon a network of substantive and formal arguments drawn from the most diverse backgrounds, such as theatre architecture, stagecraft, exhibition design, visual arts and design. Thus, this complexity of different art forms he deals with is the source of his theoretical thinking which he documented and published in the *Manifeste du Corréalisme* in the late 1940s.[1] The *Endless House* is an architect's answer to the intricate relations between man, nature and technology. Kiesler never tired of stressing his idea of architecture as biomorphic, ecological and social which was diametrically opposed to the general view at the time.[2] His many papers, publications and interviews bear eloquent witness to this. It may be for the utopian content and the wide range of substantive arguments in his theory that his big breakthrough was so long in the making. Many of the established architecture and art critics in the German-speaking area persistently ignored him until well into the 1990s.[3]

As the new European construction style gained ground in early 1930s America, Kiesler launched an attack on the rectangular, the tradition of bearing and weighing as promoted in international construction principles, and instead came up with a biomorphic self-bearing monocoque construction. His main concern was the psycho-social aspect: »On the other hand we must not – in the hope of making the house commodious – turn the process of his creation in reverse, and begin with the 'purely' aesthetic element, building in the practical and functional afterward; we must strive from the outset *to satisfy the psyche of the dweller*. Moreover, the needs of the psyche should not be repressed and projected in surface decoration. Such aestheticism is a hypocritical mask, which must eventually be cast off. Whether the mask be of concrete, glass or plastic, made to measure or prefabricated, it remains a mask and is not inwardly bound up with creative man.«[4]

This perspective of Kiesler's artistic work reflects his concern for the primary housing needs and requirements of human beings under specific circumstances: »Technological environment is produced by human needs. Investigation of this crucial point cannot be based on a study of architecture but must be based on a study of the life processes of man.«[5]

Als Friedrich Kiesler 1960 in der Ausstellung *Visionary Architecture* im Museum of Modern Art, New York sein Architekturmodell des *Endless House* präsentiert, blickt er bereits auf eine Zeitspanne von über fünfzehn Jahren der Auseinandersetzung mit diesem Ideenkonstrukt. Kieslers Arbeit am *Endless House*, der nie realisierten Idee eines Einfamilienhauses, liegt ein Netz an inhaltlicher und formaler Auseinandersetzung aus unterschiedlichen Bereichen wie Theaterarchitektur, Bühnentechnik, Ausstellungsgestaltung, bildender Kunst und Design zugrunde. Aus dieser komplexen Beschäftigung mit den verschiedenen Künsten erwächst folglich auch sein theoretisches Denken, welches er in den späten vierziger Jahren mit seinem »Manifeste du Corréalisme« niederschreibt und publiziert.[1] Das *Endless House* ist die architektonische Antwort auf das im Manifest dargelegte komplexe System an Wechselbeziehungen von Mensch, Natur und Technik. Kiesler wurde es nicht müde, immer wieder in Texten, Publikationen und Interviews eine biomorphe, ökologisch-soziale Architekturauffassung gegen den damals gängigen Diskurs zu bekräftigen.[2] Es mag an dem utopischen Gehalt und der sehr weitläufigen Anlage der verschiedenen inhaltlichen Aspekte seiner Theorie gelegen haben, dass ihm der große Durchbruch lange verwehrt blieb. Die etablierte deutschsprachige Architektur- und Kunstkritik hat ihn größtenteils bis in die neunziger Jahre beharrlich missachtet.[3] Die Ausstellung bietet daher die Gelegenheit, die Idee des *Endless House* von Friedrich Kiesler erstmals in Deutschland in einem erweiterten Umfang zugänglich zu machen.

Als sich im Amerika der frühen dreißiger Jahre der neue europäische Stil des Bauens etabliert, greift Kiesler das rektanguläre, auf der Tradition des Tragens und Lastens beruhende Bauprinzip des Internationalen Stils an und setzt ihm eine biomorphe, selbst tragende Schalenkonstruktion entgegen. Wichtig ist ihm dabei der psychosoziale Aspekt: »Wir müssen von Anfang an danach streben, *der Psyche des Bewohners Genüge zu tun*. Die Bedürfnisse der Psyche sollten nicht zurückgedrängt und auf äußere Dekorationen projiziert werden. Ein derartiger Ästhetizismus ist eine scheinheilige Maske, die früher oder später abgelegt werden muss. Ob diese Maske nun aus Beton, Glas oder Plastik, maßgefertigt oder vorfabriziert ist, sie bleibt eine Maske, sie steht nicht mit dem Innersten des kreativen Menschen in Verbindung.«[4]

Diese Ausrichtung in Kieslers künstlerischem Schaffen spiegelt die Auseinandersetzung mit den primären Bedürfnissen und Bedingungen des Wohnens von Menschen in bestimmten Situationen wider. »Das technologische Umfeld

During the 1930s and 40s, Kiesler wrote a number of publications where he developed the theory of *Correalism* as a new science that was to perceive man and his environment as a holistic system and to erase the lines between different art forms.[6] He paraphrased the *Endless House* as a germ cell, a nucleus of new forms of life and coexistence with man's mental, physical and social circumstances as the variable parameters determining and shaping his living space . »It (the being) cannot live without *others*. Its life is community. Its reality is a co-reality. Its realism is a correalism. Its reality is a realism of coordinated forces which condition, limit, push, pull, support one another; which leap together and leap apart.«[7]

As Kiesler writes in his paper »Pseudofunctionalism and Modern Architecture«: »We must not, however, put too much blame on the architect himself, because the normal curriculum of a school of architecture does not make him master of those sciences necessary for the understanding of man as a biological, psychological, socio-political being.«[8]

Kiesler's hitherto unpublished book *Magic Architecture* reveals something about the way he perceived the psychological in the context of architecture.[9] Extracts from the book have been included in this catalogue. In it, Kiesler offers a multi-facetted, experimental analysis of construction from the point of view of a cultural scientist to show how circumstances have led human beings from different cultures and animals to develop different building strategies. The book seeks to find out why human beings and animals build the way they do by looking at the biological and cultural circumstances which affect the dwellings of living beings. Kiesler's reaction to the widely accepted formula »Form follows function« was to perceive architecture as dependent on the different constellations of the mental, the physical and the reality of social circumstances in a continuously changing environment. A recurring three-part proclamation in many of his papers was that »Form does not follow function – function follows vision – vision follows reality.«[10]

Kiesler's exhibition designs of the 1940s had a major bearing on his perception of space and how it developed. He did his first sketches and studies on the *Endless House* in 1947, while he was preparing plans for *Blood Flames* at the Hugo Gallery in New York, and *Salle des Superstitions* for the *Exposition Internationale du Surréalisme* at the Galerie Maeght in Paris. His drawings and drafts show the substantive core of his theories on the psychology of space perception as a continuously changing tension in the relationship between man, art and space.

The architectural studies Kiesler did in the late 1940s manifest his ideas on architectural space design. He did studies on simple, alveolate solids as well as on multistorey residential complexes. In these he still combined cubic and organic forms, which were partly connected by corridors and shafts (see pictures 16-19) to create a sculptural effect. The laminated pieces of paper are seen as enveloping these independent architectural shapes. Around 1950, he did a series of drawings and two models for the Endless House while working on the exhibition *The Muralist and the Modern Architect* at the Kootz Gallery. The clay model (see picture 40) is a first attempt at formally implementing his idea of a »germ cell«. Relevant studies emphasize a dynamic interior space concept (see picture 42), as well as a flexible lighting system adapted to that space.[11] Kiesler later spoke of his intention to draft the Endless House as an »artificial cell«, a system incorporated into nature, during an interview with CBS. »...but it can just as well be on the

wird von menschlichen Bedürfnissen erzeugt. Eine Untersuchung dieses entscheidenden Punktes kann nicht auf einem Studium der Architektur beruhen, sondern muss auf einem Studium der Lebensabläufe des Menschen fußen.«[5]

In mehreren Veröffentlichungen der dreißiger und frühen vierziger Jahre entwickelt Kiesler die Theorie des *Correalismus* als eine neue Wissenschaft, die den Menschen und seine Umwelt als ganzheitliches System begreift und die Grenzen der Kunstgattungen aufhebt.[6] Das *Endless House* paraphrasiert Kiesler darin als Keimzelle, als Nukleus neuer Formen des Lebens und Zusammenlebens, in denen die veränderlichen Parameter der psychischen, physischen und sozialen Verfasstheit den Lebensraum mitbestimmen und gestalten. »[Ein Wesen] kann nicht ohne andere leben. Sein Leben bedeutet Gemeinschaft. Seine Realität ist eine Co-Realität. Sein Realismus ist *Correalismus*. Seine Realität ist ein Realismus aus eingespielten Kräften, die einander bedingen, eingrenzen, vorantreiben, ziehen, unterstützen; die aufeinander zu- und voneinander wegspringen.«[7]

In dem Text »Pseudofunctionalism and Modern Architecture« heißt es weiter: »Das gängige Curriculum einer Architekturschule bildet ihn [den Architekten] nicht zum Fachmann in jenen Wissenschaften aus, die für das Verständnis des Menschen als biologisches, psychologisches und soziopolitisches Wesen nötig sind.«[8]

Aufschlussreich für das Verständnis von Kieslers auf die Architektur bezogenem Begriff des Psychologischen ist das bisher unveröffentlichte Buch *Magic Architecture*.[9] Im vorliegenden Katalog werden erstmals einige Auszüge publiziert. Diese facettenreiche, experimentelle kulturwissenschaftliche Analyse des Bauens zielt ab auf die Darlegung der aus den Lebensumständen begründeten Baustrategien von Menschen verschiedener Kulturkreise sowie der Tierwelt. Es ist die Suche nach den Gründen, warum Menschen und Tiere so bauen, wie sie bauen, eine Auseinandersetzung mit den biologischen und kulturellen Umständen, die sich auf die Behausung von Lebewesen auswirken. Der gängigen Formel »Form folgt Funktion« setzt Kiesler eine Auffassung von Architektur als Abhängigkeitsmuster aus den Konstellationen des Psychischen, des Physischen und der Realität sozialer Verhältnisse in einer sich ständig verändernden Lebenswelt entgegen. In Texten proklamiert er dies als Dreisatz wie folgt: »Form folgt nicht der Funktion, Funktion folgt der Vision, Vision folgt der Realität.«[10]

Eine maßgebliche Rolle in der Entwicklung von Kieslers Raumauffassung spielen seine Ausstellungsgestaltungen in den vierziger Jahren. Die Entstehung erster Skizzen und Studien zum Konzept des *Endless House* fällt in das Jahr 1947, als Kiesler die räumliche Konzeption der Ausstellung *Blood Flames* in der Hugo Gallery in New York und der *Salle des Superstitions* zur *Exposition Internationale du Surréalisme* in der Galerie Maeght in Paris entwickelt. Zeichnungen und Entwürfe lassen den inhaltlichen Kern seiner Theorien zur Psychologie der Raumwahrnehmung als eine ständig sich verändernde Spannung in der Beziehung zwischen Mensch, Kunst und Raum erkennen.

In den Architekturstudien der späten vierziger Jahre werden Kieslers Vorstellungen von architektonischer Raumkonstruktion offensichtlich. In Studien zu einfachen, wabenartigen Raumkörpern bis hin zu mehrstöckigen Wohnkomplexen verbindet Kiesler noch kubische mit organischen Formen, die teilweise mittels Gängen und Schächten miteinander verbunden sind (Abb. 16-19) und eine skulpturale Wirkung dieser architektonischen Konstellationen hervorrufen. Aufkaschier-

5 See TV interview Kiesler/ MacAndrew, »Camera Three«, CBS 1961, as printed in the catalogue.

5 Siehe hierzu das abgedruckte Fernsehinterview zwischen Kiesler und MacAndrew, »Camera Three«, CBS 1961

6 See, amongst others, »Architecture as Biotechnique«, Report, Laboratory, School of Architecture, Columbia University, published in: Architectural Record, New York 1939

6 Siehe hierzu u. a. »Architecture as Biotechnique«, Bericht, Laboratory, School of Architecture, Columbia University, in: Architectural Record, New York 1939

7 See footnote 4

7 Siehe Anm. 4

8 Ibid.

8 Ebd.

9 Friedrich Kiesler, Magic Architecture, typescript 1940s, archive of the Frederick Kiesler Center, Vienna

9 Friedrich Kiesler, Magic Architecture, Typoskript 40er-Jahre, Archiv des Friedrich Kiesler-Zentrums, Wien

10 »Form does not follow function«, manuscript, undated, archive of the Frederick Kiesler Center, Vienna

10 »Form folgt nicht der Funktion«, Manuskript, undatiert, Archiv des Friedrich Kiesler-Zentrums, Wien

11 See »Friedrich Kiesler's Endless House and Its Psychological Lighting« as printed in the catalogue

11 Siehe den hier abgedruckten Text »Friedrich Kieslers Endless House and Its Psychological Lighting«

ground or could be floating on the water or on sand. It is reinforced concrete and it is tight, airtight, and can do almost anything and is independent of deep foundations.«[12]

In 1958, Kiesler was commissioned to do a prototype for the court of sculptures at the MoMA in New York. He produced a number of drawings and several models. The biggest, which is now in the Whitney Museum of American Art in New York, also received the biggest media coverage (see picture 4). It shows how Kiesler perceived constellations in space as interwoven organic units and thus as a spatial continuum. As he did the project for the MoMA he began to use photography, not only to document the progress he was making, but as a major tool to support him in developing the Endless House. The more he considered these numerous photographs as independent studies the more he linked them to his further drawings, enabling him to »shape space in time« (see picture 56/58).

Kiesler developed his idea of architecture on the Endless House models between 1950 and 1960, a time characterized by massive changes and upheavals as far as art and the theory of art were concerned. So far, Kiesler's work and its impact on the arts scene in New York have barely been looked into. Clearly, though, his theories and his work were the subject of many discussions among the more advanced New York artists. The artist Allan Kaprow remembers that Kiesler's theory of the »endlessness« as a concept of dynamic, process-oriented perception of space became a very interesting perspective.[13] Kiesler's connection with and affinity to John Cage and Jasper Johns, who Kiesler supplied with written material on Marcel Duchamp, as well as his relationship with Robert Rauschenberg, who incorporated a portrait of Kiesler into one of his montages, are clear evidence of how strongly he communicated with the new, self-confident generation of New York artists.[14] Kiesler was seen as a kind of father figure for progressive New York artists while his European colleagues like Hans Hofmann or Joseph Albers were losing influence over young post-war artists. American artists in general were beginning to emancipate themselves from the European art tradition.

The theoretical, architectural and artistic aspects of Frederick Kiesler's Endless House addressed above have raised a number of questions which cannot be dealt with sufficiently in this foreword. A number of texts, some of them published for the first time, as well as drawings and photographs of Kiesler's visionary ideas have been collected for this catalogue to give a fresh impetus to contemporary architecture. Both the exhibition and the catalogue are a reminder that there are many more treasures in the archives of the Frederick KieslerCenter, some of which have yet to be tapped. Time and again, Kiesler's idea of the Endless House raises questions as to his concept of space. This is true in particular for one of his key statements: »The Endless House is not amorphous, not a free-for-all form. On the contrary its construction has strict boundaries according to the scale of our living. Its shape and form are determined by inherent life forces, not by building code standards or the vagaries of décor fads.«[15]

te Papierstücke bilden eine Art Umhüllung dieser eigenständigen architektonischen Formgebilde.

Um 1950 entstehen im Zuge der Ausstellung The Muralist and The Modern Architect in der Kootz Gallery eine Reihe von Zeichnungen und zwei Modelle zum Endless House. Die Entwicklung des Ton-Modells (Abb. 40) zeigt erstmals die »Keimzelle« als mögliche formale Umsetzung seine Idee. In Studien dazu beschäftigt sich Kiesler mit einem dynamischen Innenraumkonzept (Abb. 42) sowie einem flexiblen, sich dem Raum anpassenden Beleuchtungssystem.[11] In einem späteren Interview bei CBS verweist Kiesler zudem auf seine Intention, das Endless House als »künstliche Zelle« und damit als ein der Natur inkorporiertes System zu konzipieren. »[Das Endless House] kann genauso gut ebenerdig sein, es könnte auch auf dem Wasser oder auf Sand schweben. Es ist aus Stahlbeton und kompakt, luftdicht, es kann fast alles und braucht kein tiefes Fundament.«[12]

Als Kiesler 1958 den Auftrag erhält, einen Prototyp für den Skulpturenhof des MoMA in New York zu bauen, entsteht, abgesehen von zahlreichen Zeichnungen, eine Reihe von Modellen. Das größte Modell, heute im Whitney Museum of American Art in New York, findet medial die größte Verbreitung (Abb. 4). Kiesler begreift in dem Modell die Raumkonstellationen als ineinander verwobene organische Einheiten und damit als Raumkontinuum. Mit dem Projekt für das MoMA beginnt auch das Medium der Fotografie – neben seiner Funktion zur Dokumentation der Arbeitsschritte – eine wichtige Rolle im realen Entwicklungsprozess des Endless House zu spielen. In dem Maße, wie Kiesler diese zahlreichen Fotos als eigenständige Studien begreift, werden sie an den weiteren zeichnerischen Prozess gekoppelt und ermöglichen ihm ein »Formen des Raumes in der Zeit« (Abb. 56/58).

Die Entwicklung von Kieslers Architekturidee zwischen 1950 und 1960 anhand der Modelle des Endless House fällt in eine Zeit, die künstlerisch und kunsttheoretisch von massiven Veränderungen und Umwälzungen geprägt ist. Bisher ist der Einfluss von Kieslers Arbeit auf die New Yorker Kunstszene nur sehr fragmentarisch untersucht worden. Sicher ist, dass seine Theorien und seine Arbeit in den avancierten Künstlerkreisen New Yorks durchaus diskutiert wurden. So erinnert sich der Künstler Allan Kaprow, dass Kieslers Theorie der »Endlessness« als Konzept einer dynamischen, prozessorientierten Auffassung von Raum eine interessante Perspektive darstellte.[13] Die freundschaftliche und geistige Verbundenheit Kieslers mit John Cage ebenso wie mit Jasper Johns, den Kiesler mit Texten über Marcel Duchamp versorgt, sowie die Beziehung zu Robert Rauschenberg, der in eine seiner Bildmontagen Kieslers Portrait integriert, sind Belege für den Austausch Kieslers mit der neuen, selbstbewussten Generation New Yorker Künstler.[14] Kiesler wird von progressiven Künstlern in New York als eine Art Vaterfigur angesehen, als seine europäischen Kollegen – wie etwa Hans Hofmann oder Joseph Albers – an Einfluss auf die jungen Künstler der Nachkriegszeit verlieren. Man beginnt allgemein von der Emanzipation der amerikanischen Künstler von den europäischen Kunsttraditionen zu sprechen.

An die hier kurz angerissenen theoretischen, architektonischen und künstlerischen Aspekte des Endless House von Friedrich Kiesler knüpfen sich noch zahlreiche Fragen, die hier nicht hinreichend ausgeführt werden können. Die im vorliegenden Katalog zum Teil erstmals publizierten Texte, Zeichnungen und Fotos von Kieslers visionären Konzepten sollen der zeitgenössischen Architekturentwicklung neue Impulse geben. Gleichzeitig lenken Ausstellung und Katalog die Aufmerksamkeit der Kiesler-Forschung auf die teils noch

12 See footnote 5
12 Siehe Anm. 5
13 Interview with Allan Kaprow, Vienna, June 20, 2002
13 Gespräch mit Allan Kaprow, Wien, 20. Juni 2002
14 See Kiesler's correspondence with Jasper Johns, the Museum of Modern Art in New York, as well as documents in the archive of the Frederick Kiesler Center, Vienna
14 Siehe hierzu die Korrespondenz Kieslers mit Jasper Johns, dem Museum of Modern Art New York und Dokumente im Archiv des Friedrich Kiesler-Zentrums, Wien
15 Frederick Kiesler »Notes on Architecture as Sculpture« in: Art in America, May-June 1966

unerschlossenen Bestände im Archiv des Friedrich Kiesler-Zentrums. Kieslers Idee des *Endless House* wirft in jeder Generation neue Fragen auf, die mit seinem Raumkonzept verknüpft sind. Dies gilt allein schon für einen Schlüsselsatz Kieslers: »Das *Endless House* ist nicht amorph, nicht eine Form, die frei für alles ist. Im Gegenteil, seine Konstruktion hat strenge Grenzen, entsprechend dem Maßstab unserer Lebensweise. Seine Gestalt und Form sind bestimmt durch innewohnende Lebenskräfte und nicht durch Baugesetze oder die Launen von Dekor-Marotten.«[15]

15 Friedrich Kiesler, »Notes on Architecture as Sculpture«, in: *Art in America*, Mai/Juni 1966

5 *MAGIC ARCHITECTURE*, 1940S, COVER
MAGIC ARCHITECTURE, 40ER-JAHRE, UMSCHLAG

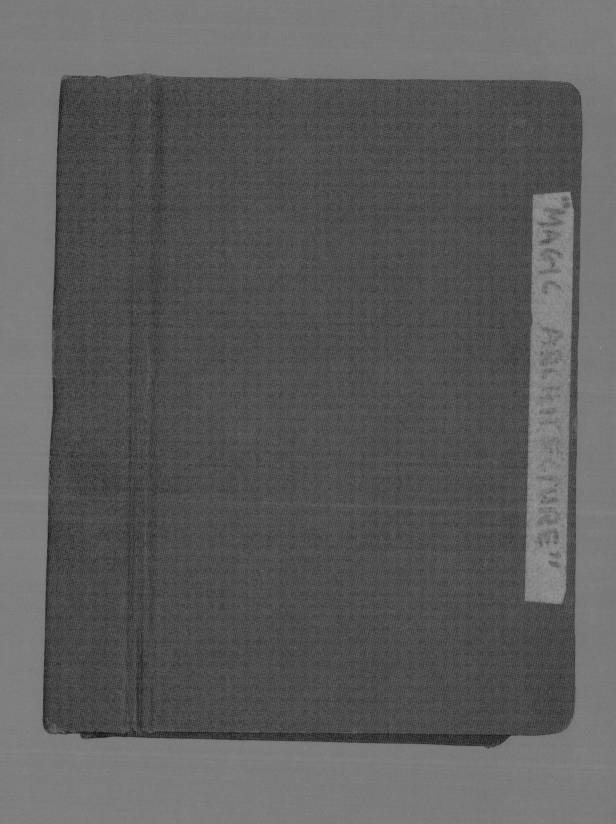

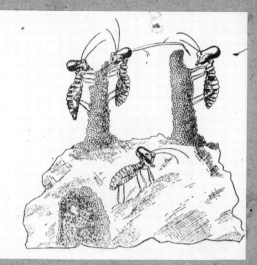

Termites building an Arch. (Arch considered to be *p.105* invention of man)
(left): Erecting two columns out of sand grains
(right): Laying a frass-stalk across the two columns, as a re-inforcement of the arch.

Similar arch-form made by man (Thermes of Caracalla, Rome, Italy)

FREDERICK KIESLER: MAGIC ARCHITECTURE[1], 1940s

Flight into the Dream World of Surrealism (Art without Architecture)

It was after the first world war; before the second was in progress, another European group developed a counter-action. Starting in literature, it flooded into painting and sculpture and into architecture by way of fantastic furnishings. They did not design houses. In the dualism of Vision and Fact, Surrealism resurrected Vision. Fact was only retained as an ingredience of man's subconscious. In truth, Vision should create out of itself, automatically. The new esthetics were anti-machine. Man's house does not matter as long as his mind is sheltered by subconsciuos living.

Flucht in die Traumwelt des Surrealismus (Kunst ohne Architektur)

Es war nach dem Ersten Weltkrieg; bevor der Zweite im Gange war, entwickelte eine weitere europäische Gruppe eine Gegenaktion. Sie nahm ihren Ausgang in der Literatur, strömte auf Malerei und Bildhauerei und mittels fantastischen Mobiliars auf die Architektur über. Sie entwarfen keine Häuser. Im Dualismus von Vision und Wirklichkeit ließ der Surrealismus die Vision auferstehen. Die Wirklichkeit blieb bloß als ein Bestandteil des menschlichen Unterbewusstseins erhalten. In Wahrheit sollte die Vision aus sich selbst heraus schöpfen, automatisch. Die neue Ästhetik war gegen die Maschine. Des Menschen Haus ist nicht von Bedeutung, solange sein Geist im unterbewussten Leben Unterschlupf findet.

(...) Just as man eats everything (meat, vegetables, fruits), he uses all the methods of house-building used by other creatures.
For example he uses:
the thatched roof and walls of birds
the concrete of termites
the earthmounds of the mole
the timber of the beaver
the netting of the spider
the standardized cell-manufacture of the bee
and the know-how of holding parts together by weaving or the use of fluids which become adhesive through drying, practises common to an infinity of creatures.
Man is a composite animal in building-materials and building-techniques.

(...) So wie der Mensch alles isst (Fleisch, Gemüse, Früchte), wendet er alle Methoden des Hausbaus anderer Geschöpfe an.
So verwendet er beispielsweise:
das Strohdach und die Strohwände der Vögel
den Beton der Termiten
die Erdhügel des Maulwurfs
das Nutzholz des Bibers
das Netz der Spinne
die genormte Zellmanufaktur der Biene
und das Know-how, Teile zu verbinden, indem man sie verwebt oder mit Flüssigkeiten benetzt, die durchs Trocknen haftend werden; Praktiken, wie unzählig viele Tiere sie anwenden.
Der Mensch vereint, was Baumaterialien und Bautechniken anbelangt, alle Tiere in sich.

1 Unpublished typescript, undated (1940s), archive of the Kiesler Center, Vienna (Text selected by Valentina Sonzogni)
1 Auszüge aus dem unveröffentlichten Typoskript *Magische Architektur*, undatiert (40er-Jahre), Archiv des Friedrich Kiesler-Zentrums, Wien (Texte ausgewählt von Valentina Sonzogni)

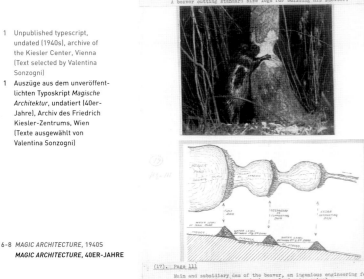

6-8 *MAGIC ARCHITECTURE*, 1940S
MAGIC ARCHITECTURE, 40ER-JAHRE

Introduction
Towards Magic Architecture

Magic Architecture is the expression of the creativeness of man. It is an architecture of contact, not of separation and resignation. Its emphasis is on participation, not on isolation; in contrast to Dream Architecture, it is not an expression of escape into religious solitude.
Magic Architecture is not dream-architecture (sic), like that of temples and castles; it is the architecture of everyday, every-night reality.

[...] Magic Architecture is a generator. It can operate on any scale. Any cell of habitation is a nucleus for a power house of joyful living. Neither wealth of cash, nor of building material, nor social power are needed to accomplish it. It follows the old rule of achieving the most with the least. It relies on self confidence, and self confidence in the discovery of natural capacities. It holds the balance between the two extremes of man: a) desire for the machine, and b) the denial of science. Its magic consists solely in the discovery of capacities in the natural ore of a being – and by refining it brings forth to the latent qualities.

Magic Architecture is, of course, unthinkable without its sociological roots in a society of free will and sacrifice. Its magic cannot be performed like the tricks of a pre stidigitator. Its power to stimulate the evolution of unheard of capacities in man, can be part only of the structure of a society devoted to such ideals. That is nothing new. Every religious community has produced extraordinary architectural developments and styles.

Einleitung
Hin zur Magischen Architektur

Die Magische Architektur ist Ausdruck der Kreativität des Menschen. Sie ist eine Architektur der Berührung, nicht der Trennung und Resignation. Sie setzt auf Mitbeteiligung, nicht auf Isolation; im Gegensatz zur Traumarchitektur ist sie nicht Ausdruck einer Flucht in andächtige Zurückgezogenheit.

[...] Die Magische Architektur ist keine Traumarchitektur wie die von Tempeln und Schlössern; sie ist die Architektur der alltäglichen, allnächtlichen Realität.
Die Magische Architektur ist ein Generator. Sie kann in jedem Maßstab arbeiten. Jede Wohnzelle ist der Nukleus für ein Kraftwerk freudigen Lebens. Es sind keine großen Mengen an Bargeld, Baumaterial oder gesellschaftlicher Macht zu ihrer Umsetzung erforderlich. Sie befolgt die alte Regel, aus wenig viel zu machen. Sie setzt auf Selbstvertrauen und Selbstvertrauen in die Entdeckung natürlichen Potenzials. Sie hält das Gleichgewicht zwischen den beiden Extremen, zwischen denen der Mensch schwankt: a) dem Wunsch nach der Maschine und b) der Ablehnung der Wissenschaft. Ihre Magie besteht einzig im Aufspüren von Kapazitäten im natürlichen Erz eines Lebewesens – und indem sie es fördert, bringt sie verborgene Eigenschaften zu Tage.

Die Magische Architektur ist natürlich undenkbar ohne ihre soziologische Verwurzelung in einer freien und gemeinnützigen Gesellschaft. Ihre Magie lässt sich nicht vorführen wie die Tricks eines Taschenspielers. Ihr Vermögen, im Menschen ungeahnte Fähigkeiten zu stimulieren, kann sich nur als Teil der Struktur einer Gesellschaft mit derartigen Idealen entfalten. Das ist nicht neu. Jede religiöse Gemeinschaft hat außergewöhnliche architektonische Entwicklungen und Stile hervorgebracht.

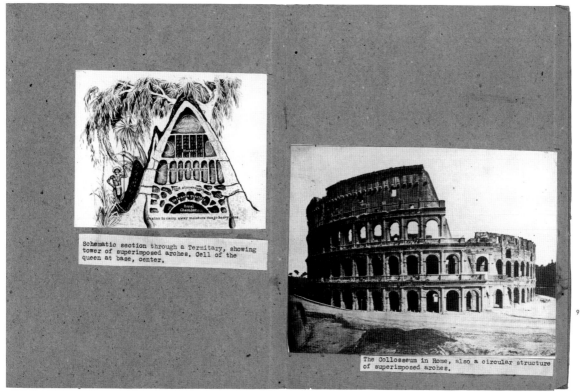

Schematic section through a Termitary, showing tower of superimposed arches. Cell of the queen at base, center.

The Collosseum in Rome, also a circular structure of superimposed arches.

9 *MAGIC ARCHITECTURE*, 1940S
MAGIC ARCHITECTURE, 40ER-JAHRE

The Nest, First Artificial Shelter

If there were no other fact to determine the descent of homo sapiens, the building methods of the primates and anthropoid apes would betray his origin. Man has indeed added nothing to the fundamentals of shelter buildings.

Shortly before nightfall (fifteen minutes before six o'clock) the orang starts the making of his nest. He stands erect, – although in a slightly stooped natural position on a forked branch, using his left arm for support; while, with his right hand he pulls towards him branches that are further away; he breaks them with his hand and heaps them crosswise to left and right, in front and behind him, until he is surrounded by a wreath of broken branches, as high as 45 centimeters or higher. This done, the orang starts preparing the ground by breaking smaller twigs and putting them in the middle of the nest. In this way the form of the nest is completed and now he starts padding it. For this purpose he grasps long branches as far back as he can reach and slide his half closed hand down the entire length of the branch so that all the leaves strip off and fall directly into the nest and collect in his hand. If the latter is the case he throws them on a certain spot in the nest and presses them into the cracks with his fist. He fills out the framework. Then the orang lays himself down sidewise, pulls towards him the fine hands of the branches and weaves them into his nest to form a dome-like covering. Here and there he breaks off a few branches and pulls them over himself so that they cover him completely. Apparently he does that to guard himself against the heavy dew and the coldness of the night.

An analysis of the material used by the orang utan (orang = man, utan = forest; forestman) and the methods of construction and the continuity in procedure,

Das Nest, die erste künstliche Behausung

Gäbe es keinen anderen Umstand, die Abstammung des Homo sapiens zu bestimmen, die Baumethoden der Primaten und Menschenaffen würden seinen Ursprung verraten. Der Mensch hat in der Tat den Grundlagen des Bauens von Behausungen nichts hinzugefügt.

Kurz vor Einbruch der Nacht (fünfzehn Minuten vor sechs Uhr) beginnt der Orang-Utan sein Nest zu bauen. Er steht aufrecht – wenn auch in leicht gebeugter Haltung – auf einer Astgabel und stützt sich auf seinen linken Arm, während er mit seiner rechten Hand Äste heranholt, die weiter weg sind; er bricht sie mit der Hand ab und häuft sie kreuzweise links und rechts, vor und hinter sich an, bis er von einem Kranz von abgebrochenen Ästen umgeben ist, der bis 45 Zentimeter oder höher hinaufreicht. Ist dies geschehen, bereitet der Orang-Utan den Boden vor, indem er kleinere Zweige zerbricht und in die Mitte des Nests legt. Wenn das Nest seine Form hat, beginnt er es auszupolstern. Zu diesem Zweck packt er lange Zweige, so weit sein Arm reicht, und lässt seine halb geschlossene Hand deren ganze Länge hinuntergleiten, sodass alle Blätter abgerissen werden und direkt ins Nest fallen, worauf er sie mit seiner Hand aufnimmt. Dann wirft er sie auf eine bestimmte Stelle des Nests und presst sie mit seinen Fäusten in die Spalten. Er füllt das Gerüst aus. Dann legt sich der Orang-Utan auf die Seite, zieht die feinen Verzweigungen der Äste zu sich heran und verwebt sie in sein Nest, um so eine kuppelartige Decke zu bilden. Hier und dort bricht er ein paar Zweige ab und legt sie über sich, sodass sie ihn vollständig bedecken. Augenscheinlich tut er das, um sich gegen den schweren Tau und die Kälte der Nacht zu wappnen.

Eine Analyse des Materials, das der Orang-Utan verwendet (orang = Mensch, utan = Wald; Waldmensch), sowie die Baumethoden und die Abfolge der Arbeitsschritte

2. Nest des Orang-Utan.

4. Nest der Zwergmaus.

1. Nest des Eichhörnchens.

10

11

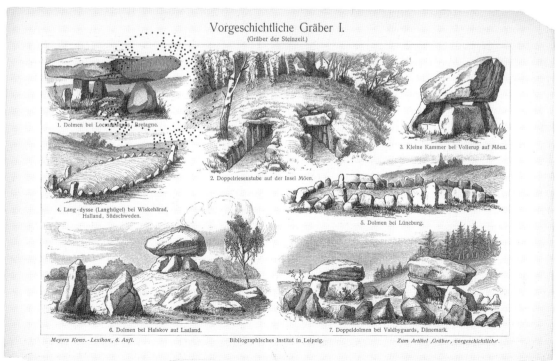

Vorgeschichtliche Gräber I.
(Gräber der Steinzeit.)

1. Dolmen bei Locmariaquer, Bretagne.

2. Doppelriesenstube auf der Insel Möen.

3. Kleine Kammer bei Vollerup auf Möen.

4. Lang-dysse (Langhügel) bei Wiskehärad, Halland, Südschweden.

5. Dolmen bei Lüneburg.

6. Dolmen bei Halskov auf Laaland.

7. Doppeldolmen bei Valdbygaards, Dänemark.

Meyers Konv.-Lexikon, 6. Aufl.   Bibliographisches Institut in Leipzig.   Zum Artikel ‚Gräber, vorgeschichtliche'.

10–11 *MAGIC ARCHITECTURE*, 1940S, RESEARCH MATERIALS
MAGIC ARCHITECTURE, 40ER-JAHRE, RECHERCHEMATERIALIEN

would easily prove that in principal there is no difference between his shelter and ours: the frame-house of our time is erected in the same way as the orang utan erects his. (...)

The other method of building enclosures which we still rely on, is that of piling stones upon each other. In doing so we are guided by our collective memory of sheltering caves, which, in truth, were nothing else but a continuous arch of stones about us. We use the stone either raw, trimmed or cut to fit, or, (when there is a lack of mud for making sun-dried brick) we pulverize stone and bring it back to life in a moulded form by mixing its powder with liquids until it hardens again, this time to a size, weight and trim we have decided upon. In this way we pride ourselves on having controlled nature and made her, at least to a certain degree, obey our wishes. And we used to do that and still do it because caves and thick foliage are not always available when we need them; and leading a life which changes according to the availability of food, we had either to take our tents with us when moving, or we had artificially to erect caves and houses when nature failed to provide them for us.

würden mit Leichtigkeit beweisen, dass im Prinzip kein Unterschied zwischen seiner Behausung und der unsrigen besteht: Das Fachwerkhaus unserer Zeit wird so errichtet, wie auch der Orang-Utan seine Behausung baut. (...)

Die andere Methode, Einfriedungen zu bauen, auf die wir uns noch immer verlassen, ist, Stein auf Stein zu setzen. Dabei werden wir von unserer kollektiven Erinnerung an schützende Höhlen geleitet, die in Wahrheit auch nichts anderes waren als ein fortlaufender Steinbogen um uns herum. Wir verwenden den Stein entweder unbehandelt, zugehauen oder zugeschnitten oder (wenn es an Schlamm für in der Sonne getrocknete Ziegel fehlt) pulverisieren den Stein und holen ihn in gegossener Form ins Leben zurück, indem wir sein Pulver mit Flüssigkeiten vermischen, bis er wieder erhärtet, dieses Mal mit der Größe, dem Gewicht und der Fasson, die wir ihm zugedacht haben. Auf diese Weise können wir uns rühmen, die Natur kontrolliert und, zumindest bis zu einem gewissen Grad, unseren Wünschen unterworfen zu haben. Und das haben wir getan und tun es noch immer, weil Höhlen und dichtes Laubwerk nicht immer verfügbar sind, wenn wir sie brauchen; und aufgrund unseres Lebens, das sich je nach Verfügbarkeit der Nahrung veränderte, mussten wir entweder unsere Zelte mit uns nehmen, wenn wir weiterwanderten, oder künstlich Höhlen und Häuser errichten, wenn die Natur keine für uns bereithielt.

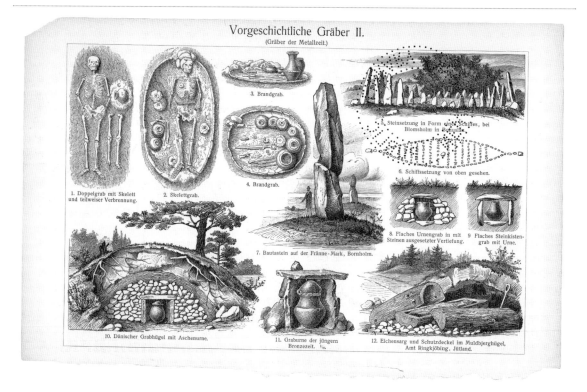

12 MAGIC ARCHITECTURE, 1940S,
RESEARCH MATERIALS
MAGIC ARCHITECTURE, 40ER-JAHRE,
RECHERCHEMATERIALIEN

13-14 MAGIC ARCHITECTURE, 1940S
MAGIC ARCHITECTURE, 40ER-JAHRE

/6 (d): A skyscraper for a hundred thousand inhabitants, relatively
four times as high as the Empire State Building, and six times as
high as:
/6 (e): the R. C. A. Building in New York City. (As compared to the
height of a white ant - 3/16 of an inch.)

(13). ~~Woodland~~ (The Forests)

(a,b): Architecture of man, small and great alike, receives and
depends on natures inspiration, her designs, construction
principles, forms and materials.
(Left): Redwoods, California, U.S.A.
(Right): Arcade of St. Peters, Rome, Italy.

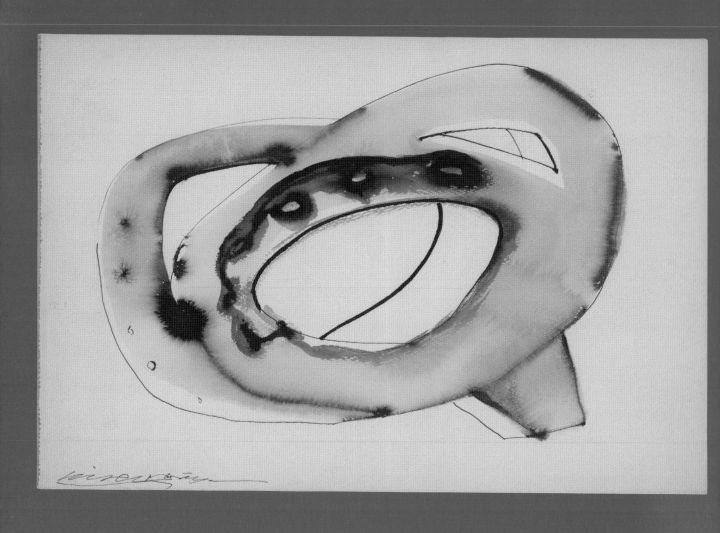

ENDLESS HOUSE 1947-1961

16

17

16 STUDIE ZU *MAISON EN TROIS D'ÉTACHES*, 1947
17–19 ARCHITEKTURSTUDIE, UM 1947

18

19

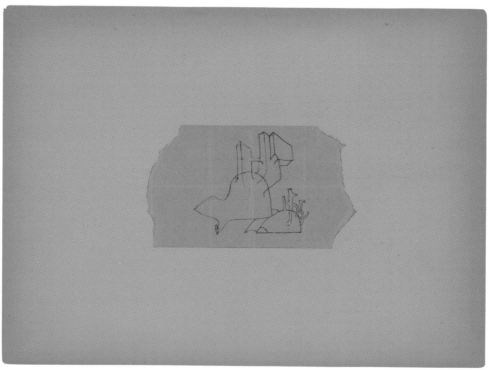

20

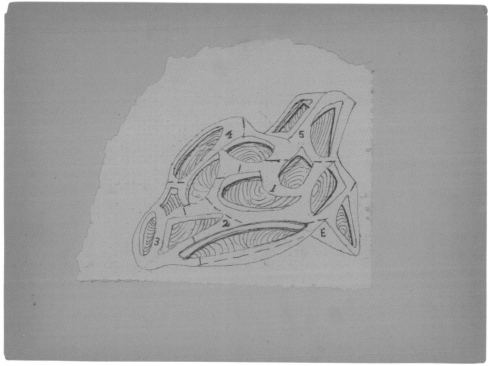

21

20–22 ARCHITEKTURSTUDIE, UM 1947

22

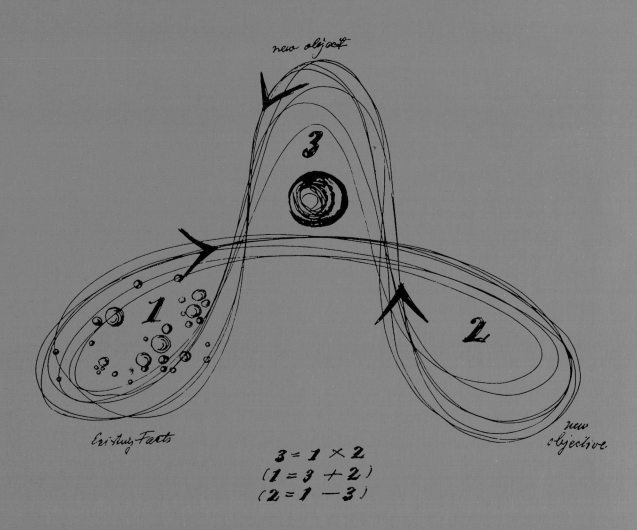

new object

3

1

2

Existing Facts

new objective.

$$3 = 1 \times 2$$
$$(1 = 3 + 2)$$
$$(2 = 1 - 3)$$

23 »CHART OF CREATION – MUTATION«,
IN: *PARTISAN REVIEW*, JULY 1949
»CHART OF CREATION – MUTATION«,
IN: *PARTISAN REVIEW*, JULI 1949

FREDERICK KIESLER:
PSEUDO-FUNCTIONALISM IN MODERN ARCHITECTURE[1]

The floor plan

The floor plan is no more than the footprint of the house. From a flat impression of this sort it is difficult to conceive the actual form and content of the building. If God had begun the creation of man with a footprint, a monster all heels and toes would probably have grown up from it, not a man. (He might have been without head and arms, to say nothing of his internal structure.) Fortunately the creation proceeded otherwise, growing out of a nuclear conception. Out of a single germ cell which contained the *whole* and which slowly developed into the separate floors and the rooms of man. This cell, owing its origin to the erotic and creative instinct and not to any intellectual mandate, is the nucleus of the human edifice. It is a strange compound; while still a gelatinous mass it contains the future man, his mind and his istinct, his sweat and his dream. It is as though nature cast the first ball into the arena of life , and then stood by folded arms to see what the play of circumstances would make of it. Whatever sort of creature results, it is never deflated, but three-dimensional, like a ball; it seeks *coordination*. With all its sense it breathes *contact*. It is connected by an infinite number of ties, bonds, rays, waves, molecular bridges, with the visible, the tangible, that which can be readily smelled and equally with that which cannot be readily smelled, that which is not immediately tangible, the invisible; and it puts forth myriad threads of its own in order to entangle itself still further in life. It cannot live without *others*. Its life is community. Its reality is a co-reality. Its realism is a correalism. Its reality is a realism of coordinated forces which condition, limit, push, pull, support one another; which leap together and leap apart like groups of acrobats in a circus, who transforms themselves from one unit, without losing their balance. In life this balance can be lost only once. And then there is no net to catch one, as in the arena. There is only death. Correalism expires.

If we had progressed to the point of working freely, that is, of creating a concrete thing free from the realities of routine, then we architects would surely not plan buildings by »drawing floor plans«; we would first of all (and I have been trying to do this for many years[2]) project on paper the nucleus of the dwelling universe: *the nervous system of the house*. At this stage we need not greatly concern ourselves with the future ears, hands and other functional organs of the body of the house, for these possibilities are of course already present in the germ cell of the initial draft. The feet of our houses, or stairs, the noses, or ventilators – all these struc-

Der Grundriss

Der Grundriss ist nichts weiter als der Fußabdruck des Hauses. Ausgehend von einem solchen zweidimensionalen Eindruck ist es schwierig, die tatsächliche Form und den tatsächlichen Inhalt eines Gebäudes zu erfassen. Hätte Gott die Erschaffung des Menschen mit einem Fußabdruck begonnen, wäre vermutlich ein Ungeheuer aus lauter Fersen und Zehen entstanden, nicht ein Mensch. (Er wäre vielleicht ohne Kopf und Arme geblieben, von seiner inneren Struktur ganz zu schweigen.) Glücklicherweise vollzog sich die Schöpfung anders und erwuchs einem Zellkern-Konzept. Aus einer einzelnen Keimzelle, die das *Ganze* enthielt und sich langsam in die verschiedenen Ebenen und Räume des Menschen entwickelte. Diese Zelle, die ihren Ursprung dem erotischen und schöpferischen Trieb und nicht irgendeinem intellektuellen Befehl verdankte, ist der Nukleus des menschlichen Gebäudes. Sie ist eine seltsame Mischung; selbst noch immer gallertige Masse, enthält sie bereits den zukünftigen Menschen, seinen Verstand und seinen Instinkt, seinen Schweiß und seinen Traum. Es ist, als hätte die Natur den ersten Ball auf das Feld des Lebens gerollt und dann mit verschränkten Armen zugesehen, was das Spiel der Umstände aus ihm machen würde. Welches Wesen auch immer daraus hervorgeht, es ist niemals flach, sondern dreidimensional, wie ein Ball; es sucht nach *Koordination*. Mit all seinen Sinnen lechzt es nach *Kontakt*. Es ist durch unendlich viele Beziehungen, Bindungen, Strahlen, Wellen und molekulare Brücken verbunden mit dem Sichtbaren, dem Greifbaren, dem leicht Riechbaren und gleichermaßen mit dem nicht leicht Riechbaren, dem nicht unmittelbar Greifbaren, dem Unsichtbaren; und es streckt seinerseits Myriaden von Fäden aus, um sich noch tiefer im Leben zu verankern. Es kann nicht ohne *andere* leben. Sein Leben bedeutet Gemeinschaft. Seine Realität ist eine Co-Realität. Sein Realismus ist Correalismus. Seine Realität ist ein Realismus aus eingespielten Kräften, die einander bedingen, eingrenzen, vorantreiben, ziehen, unterstützen; die aufeinander zu und voneinander weg springen wie Akrobaten in einem Zirkus; die sich aus einer Formation heraus verwandeln, ohne das Gleichgewicht zu verlieren. Im Leben kann man diese Balance nur einmal verlieren. Und dann gibt es kein Netz, das einen auffängt wie in der Zirkusarena. Sondern nur den Tod. Der Correalismus erlischt.

Wären wir bereits an den Punkt gelangt, frei zu arbeiten, das heißt, Konkretes frei von den Sachzwängen der Routine zu schaffen, dann würden wir Architekten Gebäude gewiss nicht entwerfen, indem wir »Grundrisse zeichnen«; wir wür-

1 »Pseudo-Functionalism in Modern Architecture«, in: *Partisan Review*, July 1949. Following notes are by Kiesler himself.

1 »Pseudo-Functionalism in Modern Architecture« in: *Partisan Review*, Juli 1949. Die folgenden Fußnoten stammen von Kiesler persönlich.

tural units have today once more been technically well solved (as in pharaonic Egypt or in Renaissance Italy) – these elements are available; they can be had for money. What cannot be bought is the character of the species. This must be invented. And in order to achieve it, all the creative instinct of the individual who takes it upon himself to be an architect is needed. »Modernized« tradition is not enough. Himself a being which does not consist only of muscle, bone and fluid – an architect should conceive of a new house not as mere walls and roof with a heating and cooling system, but as a living organism with the reactivity of a full-blooded creature. The house is not a digestive apparatus. Man is a nucleus of natural forces, living in emotions and dreams, through the medium of his physique. Every millimeter of his physical environment is inspiration, not merely mechanical contact. But this aesthetic needs cannot be lastingly satisfied by pictures, carpets, tapestries and candelabra intended to make his house »livable«.

On the other hand we must not –in the hope of making the house commodious– turn the process of his creation in reverse, and begin with the »purely« aesthetic element, building in the practical and functional afterward; we must strive from the outset *to satisfy the psyche of the dweller*. Moreover, the needs of the psyche should not be repressed and projected in surface decoration. Such aestheticism is a hypocritical mask, which must eventually be cast off. Whether the mask be of concrete, glass or plastic, made to measure or prefabricated, it remains a mask and is not inwardly bound up with creative man.

Man's living needs are simple. They become complicated and hypocritical only as a result of artificial stimulations – in architecture as elsewhere. Honest building can be done in wood, mud and stone, just as dishonest building can be done with alpha glass and beta aluminium.

The individual as well as the couple and the large family can adapt himself by *natural will* and instinct to unfavorable physical conditions (cathedrals were build by slum dwellers), but they cannot submit for long to unfavorable *psychic conditions*. Under certain circumstances they will ultimately leave the finest windowframe (admitting no draft), the best-laid (highly polished) floors, and withdraw to a cave in order to be free and happy. »Technical perfection« is never achieved. It is at once dream and nightmare. Only the free artist can be »perfect« in his painting or sculpture and produce something final. The technician is the slave of »progress«; consequently his perfection is only ostensible and largely a matter of circumstances. Such perfection is conditional; the work of art alone is unconditional. Technology (and especially the technology of machines) is entirely relative, or rather, correlative.

The law of creative transmutation
Functionalism is determinism and therefore stillborn. Functionalism is the standardization of routine activity. For example: a foot that walks (but does not dance); an eye that sees (but does not envision); a hand that grasps (but does not create).

Functionalism relieves the architect of responsibility to his concept. He mechanizes in terms of the current inherited conception of the practical, and little more; only simplifying and rendering ascetic (sic) what is already traditional. Actually, however, he does violence to the freedom and self-realization of the basic functions of living man.

The species is known by the total coordination of its functions, not by its esophagus.

den zuallererst (und ich versuche das seit vielen Jahren[2]) den Nukleus des »Wohn-Universums« zu Papier bringen: *das Nervensystem des Hauses*. In diesem Stadium brauchen wir uns noch nicht übermäßig mit den künftigen Ohren, Händen und anderen Funktionsorganen des Hauskörpers zu belasten, denn diese Möglichkeiten sind natürlich bereits in der Keimzelle des ersten Entwurfs angelegt. Die Füße unseres Hauses oder Treppen, die Nasen oder Ventilatoren – diese strukturellen Einheiten sind heutzutage technisch gut gelöst (wie auch schon im Ägypten der Pharaonen oder im Renaissance-Italien) – die Elemente sind verfügbar; sie sind für Geld zu haben. Was man nicht kaufen kann, ist der Charakter der Spezies. Dieser muss erfunden werden. Und zu diesem Zweck ist der ganze kreative Instinkt des Individuums, das Architekt sein will, gefordert. »Modernisierte« Tradition ist nicht genug. Als Wesen, das nicht nur aus Muskeln, Knochen und Flüssigkeit besteht, sollte ein Architekt ein neues Haus nicht nur als Mauern und Dach mit einem Heiz- und Kühlsystem begreifen, sondern als einen lebenden Organismus mit den Reaktionen einer vollblütigen Kreatur. Das Haus ist kein Verdauungsapparat. Der Mensch ist ein Nukleus natürlicher Kräfte, der über das Medium seines Körpers seine Emotionen und Träume auslebt. Jeder Millimeter seiner physischen Umgebung ist Inspiration und nicht bloß mechanischer Kontakt. Doch diese ästhetischen Bedürfnisse können auf Dauer nicht mit den Bildern, Teppichen, Tapisserien und Lüstern, die sein Haus »lebenswert« machen sollen, befriedigt werden.

Andererseits dürfen wir – in der Hoffnung, das Haus geräumig und angenehm zu machen – seinen Entstehungsprozess nicht umkehren und beim »rein« ästhetischen Element beginnen, indem wir Praktisches und Funktionelles erst im Nachhinein einbauen; wir müssen von Anfang an danach streben, *der Psyche des Bewohners Genüge zu tun*. Die Bedürfnisse der Psyche sollten nicht zurückgedrängt und auf äußere Dekorationen projiziert werden. Ein derartiger Ästhetizismus ist eine scheinheilige Maske, die früher oder später abgelegt werden muss. Ob diese Maske nun aus Beton, Glas oder Plastik, maßgefertigt oder vorfabriziert ist, sie bleibt eine Maske, sie steht nicht mit dem Innersten des kreativen Menschen in Verbindung.

Die Lebensbedürfnisse des Menschen sind einfach. Kompliziert und scheinheilig werden sie nur als Resultat künstlicher Stimulationen – in der Architektur wie überall sonst. Ehrlich bauen kann man mit Holz, Lehm und Stein, genauso wie man mit Alpha-Glas und Beta-Aluminium unehrlich bauen kann.

Das Individuum kann sich, wie auch das Paar und die Großfamilie, durch *natürlichen Willen* und Instinkt widrigen physischen Bedingungen anpassen (Kathedralen wurden von den Bewohnern von Elendsvierteln erbaut), doch sie können nicht lange unter widrigen *psychischen Bedingungen* bestehen. Unter bestimmten Umständen werden sie letztlich den schönsten Fensterrahmen (der keine Zugluft durchlässt), die optimalst verlegten (auf Hochglanz polierten) Böden hinter sich lassen und sich in eine Höhle zurückziehen, um frei und glücklich zu sein. »Technische Perfektion« wird nie erreicht. Sie ist Träum und Albtraum zugleich. Einzig der freie Künstler kann in seiner Malerei oder Bildhauerei »perfekt« sein und Endgültiges hervorbringen. Der Techniker ist Sklave des »Fortschritts«; folglich ist seine Perfektion nur vorgeblich und größtenteils eine Frage der Umstände. Eine solche Perfektion ist immer von Bedingungen abhängig; das Kunstwerk allein ist bedingungslos. Technologie (und insbesondere die Maschinentechnologie) ist ganz und gar relativ, oder vielmehr correlativ.

2   See designs for the *Endless*, Paris 1925, reproduced in: *Architectural Record*, 1931; *Space House*, in: *Architectural Record*, 1935; *Salle des Superstitions*, in: *L'Architecture d'Aujourd'hui*, Paris, April 1949

2   Siehe Designs for the *Endless*, Paris 1925, neu abgedruckt in: *Architectural Record*, 1931; *Space House*, in: *Architectural Record*, 1935; *Salle des Superstitions*, in: *L'Architecture d'Aujourd'hui*, Paris, April 1949

3 Two clear examples of the direct influence of abstract painting on the architecture of Corbusier and Mies van der Rohe can be found in: »Cubism and Abstract Art«, published by the Museum of Modern Art, New York 1939.

3 Zwei klare Beispiele für den direkten Einfluss der abstrakten Malerei auf die Architektur von Corbusier und Mies van der Rohe finden sich in »Cubism and Abstract Art«, publiziert vom Museum of Modern Art, New York 1939

4 »Architecture as Biotechnique«, report of the Laboratory, School of Architecture, Columbia University, in: *Architectural Record*, New York 1939

4 »Architecture as Biotechnique«, Bericht, Laboratory, School of Architecture, Columbia University, in: *Architectural Record*, New York 1939

Modern functionalism in architecture has its roots far more in contemporary abstract painting then in the »functionalism of living«[3]. And the curved forms that are now appearing in furniture and buildings, did not originate in »psychological« functionalism but in the formal idiom of Surrealism. Some architects have confused geometric forms with abstraction, have taken simplicity (or planimetry) for functionalism, and called it »organic architecture«. It was a stroke of luck that »abstract simplicity« fitted in with the principles of hygiene, fostered at that time by industry and labor.

In reality the true functionalist will accept no standard as final. He lives through the existing standard, and by this experience becomes independent of the standard as such. Then by the force of this constant materialism (1) and of his imagination which has thus been liberated, he crystallizes the new objective (2) and the new object (3). Not only does he now gradually come to master the conditions amid (sic) which his new object must be born, but through his new, real objects, he changes the conditions themselves (see *Metabolism Chart Home Library*[4]). The new idea has now become material (1) and the creative cycle begins anew.

By a change in the preponderance of the life-forces, the center of interest and attraction may shift from material fact (1) to the idea (2), from the idea – to the object (3); and in this continuous flux any other shift of emphasis is equally possible.

Thus two of three components always assume a secondary place in the total structure, and even the potential relation between these two will vary according to their correlative position. Nevertheless the strength of all three components can never be equal, for if it were, continuity would end in a static balance. The process of rebirth would be impossible. It would seem that perfect balance cannot exist in nature, and ultimately one force must become predominant over another. Thus »function« appears not as a finite fact or standard, but as a process of continuous transmutation.

Form does not follow function.
Form follows vision.
Vision follows reality.

The »abstract functionalist« was a master of self-deception. With the honesty of a fanatic he deceived his fellowmen (clients) and himself, by »improving« on the »accredited« standard of function along more abstract or super-fantastic lines, without realizing that the function which his work represents is, in spite of technical and decorative improvements, still the old hereditary residue. Modern lampshades could never »improve« on the function of the oil lamp to the point where kerosene would become electricity and a wick the filament of a light-bulb. Any improvement on an obsolete form or function ultimately arrives at its own dead end; the new cannot be grafted on the obsolescent, for it has other functional roots, i.e. obsolescence and rebirth.

They all speak of functionalism, but they have forgotten to define the world of latent functions, that is, to examine the validity of existing functions, to find new functions and eliminate obsolete ones. More glass and light, flowers on the floor instead of on a window sill, combination living and dining rooms, do not do the job. They wish to do a new architecture out of pseudo-functions, but all they do in reality is to consolidate the bank account of their professional aura.

We must not, however, put too much blame on the architect himself, because the normal curriculum of a school of architecture does not make him master of those sciences necessary for the understanding of man as a biological,

Das Gesetz der kreativen Umwandlung

Funktionalismus ist Determinismus und somit tot geboren. Funktionalismus ist die Normung von Routineabläufen. Zum Beispiel: ein Fuß, der geht (jedoch nicht tanzt); ein Auge, das sieht (sich jedoch nichts vorstellt); eine Hand, die ergreift (jedoch nicht erschafft).

Funktionalismus entgebt den Architekten der Verantwortung für sein Konzept. Er mechanisiert eine übernommene Vorstellung von dem, was gerade als praktisch gilt, und nicht viel mehr; er vereinfacht und verschönt nur, was bereits traditionell ist. Tatsächlich tut er jedoch der Freiheit und Selbstverwirklichung des wohnenden Menschen Gewalt an.

Die Spezies erkennt man am totalen Zusammenspiel ihrer Funktionen, nicht an ihrer Speiseröhre.

Moderner Funktionalismus in der Architektur wurzelt weit mehr in der zeitgenössischen abstrakten Malerei als im »Funktionalismus des Lebens«.[3] Und die gerundeten Formen, die derzeit bei Möbeln und Gebäuden Einzug halten, entspringen nicht dem »psychologischen« Funktionalismus, sondern dem formalen Idiom des Surrealismus. Manche Architekten haben geometrische Formen mit Abstraktion verwechselt, Einfachheit (oder Planimetrie) für Funktionalismus gehalten und nannten das »organische Architektur«. Was für ein Glück, dass »abstrakte Schlichtheit« zu den damals bei Industrie und Arbeiterschaft gehegten Prinzipien von Hygiene passte.

In Wirklichkeit akzeptiert der wahre Funktionalist keinen Standard als endgültigen. Er erlebt den bestehenden Standard und emanzipiert sich dank dieser Erfahrung vom Standard als solchem. Mittels dieses konstanten Materialismus (1) und seiner somit befreiten Vorstellungskraft gibt er dem neuen Ziel (2) und dem neuen Objekt (3) konkrete Form. Es gelingt ihm nun nicht nur nach und nach, die Bedingungen zu meistern, unter denen sein neues Objekt geboren werden muss, sondern er verändert durch seine neuen, faktischen Objekte eben diese Bedingungen (siehe *Metabolism Chart Home Library*[4]). Die neue Idee ist zum Material geworden (1), der Schöpfungszyklus beginnt von neuem.

Durch eine Verschiebung der Gewichtung der Lebenskräfte kann sich das Zentrum von Interesse und Anziehung von einer materiellen Tatsache (1) zur Idee (2) verlagern, von der Idee – zum Objekt (3); durch dieses ständige Fließen ist jede andere Verlagerung der Betonung ebenso möglich.

Somit nehmen zwei der drei Komponenten immer einen untergeordneten Platz in der Gesamtstruktur ein, und selbst die potenzielle Beziehung zwischen diesen beiden variiert je nach ihrer correlativen Position. Dennoch können alle drei Komponenten nie gleich stark sein, denn wenn dem so wäre, würde die Kontinuität in einem statischen Gleichgewicht enden. Der Prozess der Wiedergeburt wäre unmöglich. Es scheint, dass es in der Natur kein perfektes Gleichgewicht geben kann, und letzten Endes muss eine Kraft über eine andere dominieren. Somit erscheint »Funktion« nicht als genau umrissene Tatsache oder Standard, sondern als Prozess ständiger Umwandlung.

Die Form folgt nicht der Funktion.
Die Form folgt der Vision.
Die Vision folgt der Wirklichkeit.

Der »abstrakte Funktionalist« war ein Meister der Selbsttäuschung. Mit der Ehrlichkeit eines Fanatikers betrog er seine Mitmenschen (Kunden) und sich selbst, indem er den »anerkannten« Funktionsstandard auf abstrakten oder super-fantastischen Wegen »verbesserte«, ohne zu erkennen, dass

psychological, socio-political being. The architect's education of today is still professionally isolationist.

The position of the architect as a »worker for others« is even more difficult than that of the social planner, who stands close to him in the matter of structural principles; for in the morphology of the »technical environment« the architect combines the laws of society with exigencies of a physical order as well as the psychic influences of individuals; moreover, in attempting to realize his plans, he must lean on the techniques of other specialists, such as engineers, sculptors, painters and diverse artisans of the building trades. Although the »architect« shares his work with so many, he carries by far the greatest part of the responsibility, for neither he nor the other technicians are going to live in the house they are building, but some anonymous citizen who trusts that the home which other hands are building for him will be a healthy place to live in.

Which of us architects dares to assume *not* the aesthetic but the full moral responsibility for a building? What architect has enjoyed the training that will give him sufficient understanding of the human morphology for which he is building? Architecture today is neither science, craft, nor art. Measured by progress in the social sciences and in technical invention, we draftsmen are still architectosauruses.

Direct and indirect building
Functional architecture is animal-architecture, i.e. it produces structures for physical shelter. But animals build more economically, since they merely repeat the tradition of the species, that lies in their blood. Man is always dissatisfied, because he wants to lead the life of a master and is therefore eternally searching for new materials, implements and machines to serve as his slaves. Instead of relying on himself, man relies on progress.

A house must be practical. To be practical means to serve. To be serviceable in every respect. In every direction. If any directions are closed, the house suffers from constipation. But how can a house be practical if the draftsman always begins with the flat ground plan. Our vision is physically flat – we see with one eye (mono dimensionally) rather than stereoscopically, with two eyes, as a living spatial vision would require.

The ground plan is only a flat imprint of a volume. The volume of the principal activity to be expected in the house is not taken into consideration; instead, squares and rectangles, long ones, short ones, bent ones, are juxtaposed, or something jumbled – and then superimposed in storeys (elevation plan). This box construction is not in keeping with the practice of living. A house is a volume in which people live polydimensionally. It is the sum of every possible movement its inhabitants can make within it; and these movements in turn are imbued with the flux of instinct.

Hence it is fallacious to begin with a floor plan. We must strive to capture a *general sense* of dwelling, and configurate accordingly. This is difficult but not impossible. It is difficult, if only because the space of the house is polydimensional, and as such real, while the design cannot be (but) two-dimensional (it is imprisoned on paper so to speak). But if the design is intrinsically two-dimensional, that is all the more reason why we must not see two-dimensionally, or feel two-dimensionally *a priori*.

Primitive, prehistoric man drew no ground plans for his house. He drew no architectural design whatsoever. Not even with his finger in the sand or mud. He built *directly*. He formed space directly into a house. And from the very first peg (or block) he already lived in it. By the time the last stone

die Funktion, die sein Werk repräsentiert, bei allen technischen und dekorativen Verbesserungen noch immer dasselbe alte Erbstück ist. Moderne Lampenschirme konnten die Funktion der Öllampe nie dahin gehend »verbessern«, dass Kerosin zu Strom wurde und ein Docht zum Faden einer Glühbirne. Jede Verbesserung einer obsoleten Form oder Funktion landet schließlich in ihrer eigenen Sackgasse; das Neue kann nicht auf das Überholte aufgepfropft werden, haben sie doch verschiedene funktionale Wurzeln, nämlich Veralten und Wiedergeburt.

Alle sprechen von Funktionalismus, aber sie haben vergessen, die Welt der latenten Funktionen zu definieren, das heißt, die Gültigkeit bestehender Funktionen zu überprüfen, neue Funktionen zu finden und obsolete zu eliminieren. Mehr Glas und Licht, Blumen auf dem Boden anstatt auf dem Fenstersims, kombinierte Wohn- und Esszimmer sind nicht die Lösung. Sie möchten aus Pseudofunktionen heraus eine neue Architektur schaffen, in Wirklichkeit konsolidieren sie jedoch nur das Bankkonto ihrer professionellen Aura.

Wir dürfen jedoch nicht dem Architekten selbst zu viel Schuld geben, denn das gängige Curriculum einer Architekturschule bildet ihn nicht zum Fachmann in jenen Wissenschaften aus, die für das Verständnis des Menschen als biologisches, psychologisches und soziopolitisches Wesen nötig sind. Die heutige Ausbildung des Architekten ist noch immer ein professioneller Elfenbeinturm.

Die Position des Architekten als »Arbeiter für andere« ist sogar noch problematischer als die des Sozialplaners, der mit ähnlichen strukturellen Prinzipien befasst ist wie jener; denn in der Morphologie des »technischen Umfelds« kombiniert der Architekt gesellschaftliche Gesetze mit Anforderungen materieller Natur ebenso wie mit individuellen psychischen Einflüssen; zudem muss er sich bei der Verwirklichung seiner Pläne auf die Techniken anderer Spezialisten stützen wie zum Beispiel Ingenieure, Bildhauer, Maler und verschiedene Handwerker aus dem Baugewerbe. Obwohl der »Architekt« seine Arbeit mit so vielen teilt, trägt er den weitaus größten Teil der Verantwortung, denn weder er noch die anderen Techniker werden in dem Haus leben, das sie bauen, sondern ein anonymer Bürger, der darauf vertraut, dass das Heim, das andere Hände für ihn errichten, ein gesunder Ort zum Wohnen sein wird.

Wer von uns Architekten hat den Mut, *nicht* nur die ästhetische, sondern die volle moralische Verantwortung für ein Gebäude zu übernehmen? Welcher Architekt ist in den Genuss einer Ausbildung gekommen, die ihm ein ausreichendes Verständnis der Morphologie des Menschen, für den er baut, verleiht? Heutige Architektur ist weder Wissenschaft noch Handwerk noch Kunst. Gemessen am Fortschritt der Sozialwissenschaften und technischen Erfindungen sind wir Zeichner noch immer Architektur-Saurier.

Direktes und indirektes Bauen
Funktionelle Architektur ist Architektur für animalische Bedürfnisse, das heißt sie produziert Strukturen zum Schutz des Körpers. Doch Tiere bauen ökonomischer, da sie lediglich die Tradition der Spezies wiederholen, die ihnen im Blut liegt. Der Mensch ist immer unzufrieden, weil er das Leben eines Herrschenden führen will und deshalb immer auf der Suche nach neuen Materialien, Werkzeugen und Maschinen ist, die ihm als Sklaven dienen sollen. Statt sich auf sich selbst zu verlassen, verlässt sich der Mensch auf den Fortschritt.

Ein Haus muss praktisch sein. Praktisch sein heißt, seinen Zweck erfüllen. In jeder Hinsicht zweckmäßig sein. In

or the last leaf was laid in place, the house had already been experienced, tested. In short, the inhabitants gradually put on the house; as one might put on garments until covered.

a) The mechanization of dwelling construction proceeded roughly as follows:
b) Primitive man builds directly – without design – for himself and his family.
c) The semi-civilized man builds directly – still without plans –, but he builds also for other families.
d) »Civilized« man builds for others, people of means, and submits sketches to help sell his products. He becomes a specialist, a master builder for himself and others; he designs and also builds.
e) The machine man only designs, he no longer builds but leaves the building to other specialists; he no longer builds for himself but only for others; this is the architect of today. Possible future development: the architect no longer designs the house himself. It is collectively planned (by a group of specialists in construction, mechanized equipment and decoration), collectively built – and administered.

The social standardization has given rise to a standardization not only of the parts of houses, but of architectural forms as well.

If the standardization of architectural elements resulted from scientific knowledge (as in the case of machine construction) there would be no present objection; but since (even in the fabrication of steel rail profile) the measurements, weight and joints of the parts *are derived from previous architectural projects* (and not from a study of life processes and the needs they create), the resultant home is not an organic *whole* but a *conglomerate*. After the floors, walls and ceilings are in place, man is invited to orient himself in this vacuum and to make himself as comfortable as he can (with the help of furniture and of decoration). The architect-designer has never lived in this house, he has no experience of living in the place, and there is no architectural laboratory existent where he can observe man in an architectural environment. The experience is left to the dweller when it is too late to make fundamental changes. The present dweller who (in contrast to primitive man) never builds his own house or plans it, is completely subjected to the dictatorship of the architect and building contractor. The dweller of today has become an architectural slave.

It is difficult in a brief space to make the confusion prevailing in the construction industry clear to the layman (or to the average architect). There is a general prudery that prevents people from looking too closely into great technical achievements or institutions (the same air of secrecy surrounded the sex-life of our grandparents). Nevertheless the Euclidean system has been replaced, and recently the electric light bulb has given way to the fluorescent tube. The public accepts new philosophies much more easily, largely because people never have time to study them closely, and because they think that these philosophies are too far removed from »real life« to be dangerous.

But we must not forget that the specialization of occupation has brought with it a vast decline of general knowledge. If industry produces so much today, it is mainly for the sake of investments. Industry does not serve basic needs but turns out repetitions or stylish modifications or commodities that have proved salable. Architects and draftsmen are its unsuspecting accomplices.

jede Richtung. Wenn irgendeine Richtung blockiert ist, leidet das Haus an Verstopfung. Aber wie kann ein Haus praktisch sein, wenn der Zeichner immer vom zweidimensionalen Grundriss ausgeht? Unsere Sicht ist physisch bedingt plan – wir sehen mit einem Auge (monodimensional) statt stereoskopisch, mit zwei Augen, wie es eine lebendige räumliche Sehweise erfordern würde.

Der Grundriss ist nur der flache Abdruck eines Volumens. Das Volumen der im Haus zu erwartenden Hauptaktivität wird nicht berücksichtigt; stattdessen werden Quadrate und Rechtecke, lange, kurze, gebogene, nebeneinander gesetzt oder durcheinander gewürfelt – und dann in Etagen aufgestockt (Aufriss). Diese Schachtelkonstruktion entspricht nicht der Praxis des Lebens. Ein Haus ist ein Volumen, in dem Menschen mehrdimensional leben. Es ist die Summe aller möglichen Bewegungen, die seine Bewohner in seinem Inneren ausführen können; und diese Bewegungen sind ihrerseits erfüllt vom Fließen des Instinkts.

Daher ist es irrig, mit einem Grundriss zu beginnen. Wir müssen danach streben, ein *allgemeines Gefühl* für das Wohnen zu gewinnen, und dementsprechend gestalten. Das ist schwierig, aber nicht unmöglich. Es ist schwierig, wenn auch bloß deshalb, weil der Raum des Hauses polydimensional und somit real ist, während der Entwurf nur zweidimensional sein kann (er ist sozusagen auf dem Papier gefangen). Doch wenn der Entwurf an sich zweidimensional ist, ist das nur ein Grund mehr, warum wir nicht *a priori* zweidimensional sehen oder zweidimensional fühlen dürfen.

Der primitive, prähistorische Mensch zeichnete keine Grundrisse für sein Haus. Er zeichnete keinen wie auch immer gearteten Bauplan. Nicht einmal mit seinem Finger in den Sand oder Schlamm. Er baute *direkt*. Er formte Raum direkt zu einer Behausung. Und vom ersten Pflock (oder Block) an lebte er bereits darin. Wenn der letzte Stein oder das letzte Blatt an Ort und Stelle gelegt wurde, war das Haus bereits erprobt, getestet. Kurz, die Bewohner legten sich das Haus schrittweise um; wie man in Kleidungsstücke schlüpft, bis man sich vollständig bedeckt hat.

Die Mechanisierung des Wohnbaus vollzog sich grob umrissen folgendermaßen:

a) Der Urmensch baut direkt – ohne Entwurf – für sich selbst und seine Familie.
b) Der halb zivilisierte Mensch baut direkt – noch immer ohne Pläne –, aber er baut auch für andere Familien.
c) Der »zivilisierte« Mensch baut für andere, vermögende Leute und legt Skizzen vor, um sein Produkt besser zu verkaufen. Er wird Spezialist, ein Baumeister für sich selbst und andere; er entwirft und baut auch.
d) Der Maschinen-Mensch entwirft nur, er baut nicht mehr, sondern überlässt das Bauen anderen Spezialisten; er baut nicht mehr für sich selbst, sondern nur noch für andere; das ist der Architekt von heute.
e) Mögliche zukünftige Entwicklung: Der Architekt entwirft das Haus nicht länger selbst. Es wird kollektiv geplant (von einem Team von Spezialisten für Bauwesen, mechanisierte Einrichtung und Ausstattung), kollektiv gebaut – und verwaltet.

Die gesellschaftliche Normierung hat nicht nur zu einer Normung der Hausteile, sondern auch zu einer Vereinheitlichung der Architekturformen geführt.

Wäre die Normung architektonischer Elemente ein Resultat wissenschaftlicher Erkenntnisse (wie im Fall des Maschinenbaus), gäbe es keinen gegenwärtigen Einwand; doch weil

Via Apea

Man is an acrobatic animal that finally succeeded in standing on its hind legs, but his mind still crawls on all fours. He should know that all the devices he arrives at through his intellect have long been perceived by the vision of poets. To prove this there is no need to invoke the ideas of a Leonardo da Vinci or the writings of a Cyrano de Bergerac (who in 1640 described the phonograph). Poetry since the earliest times bears witness.

The misery of man lies far deeper: in his inability to construct anything that has not been experienced by the imagination.
He is utterly caught in the net of his imagination.
Nature holds him as a hostage.
If he could break through this net – he would be free.
But man travels the Apean way. It is his destiny to ape.
At best to ape himself. To realize his own visions mechanically.

(selbst bei der Herstellung von Stahlschienenprofilen) Maße, Gewicht und Verbindungen der Teile *von früheren Architekturprojekten hergeleitet werden* (und nicht von einem Studium der Lebensprozesse und der von ihnen hervorgerufenen Bedürfnisse), ist das daraus entstehende Haus kein organisches *Ganzes*, sondern ein *Konglomerat*. Nachdem die Böden, Wände und Decken errichtet sind, wird der Mensch eingeladen, sich in diesem Vakuum zurechtzufinden und es sich (mithilfe von Möbeln und Ausstattung) so gemütlich zu machen wie möglich. Der Architekt-Designer hat nie in diesem Haus gelebt, er hat keinen Erfahrungswert, wie es ist, hier zu wohnen, und es gibt kein Architekturlabor, in dem er den Menschen in einem architektonischen Umfeld beobachten kann. Diese Erfahrung bleibt dem Bewohner überlassen, wenn es zu spät ist, grundlegende Veränderungen vorzunehmen. Der Bewohner von heute, der (im Gegensatz zum Menschen der Urzeit) nie sein eigenes Haus baut oder plant, ist der Diktatur von Architekt und Bauunternehmer vollkommen ausgeliefert. Der Bewohner von heute ist ein Sklave der Architektur geworden.

Es ist schwierig, in Kürze die in der Bauindustrie herrschende Verwirrung dem Laien (oder dem durchschnittlichen Architekten) klar zu machen. Die Leute haben im Allgemeinen große Scheu davor, technische Errungenschaften oder Institutionen zu genau zu hinterfragen (dieselbe Heimlichtuerei umgab auch das Liebesleben unserer Großeltern). Dennoch wurde das Euklidische System abgelöst, und vor kurzem wich auch die elektrische Glühbirne der Leuchtstoffröhre. Die Öffentlichkeit akzeptiert neue Philosophien viel leichter, größtenteils, weil die Leute nie die Zeit haben, sich intensiv mit ihnen auseinander zu setzen, und weil sie diese Philosophien für zu abgehoben vom »wahren Leben« halten, um gefährlich zu sein.

Wir dürfen jedoch nicht vergessen, dass die Spezialisierung der Berufe eine große Verminderung des Allgemeinwissens mit sich gebracht hat. Wenn die Industrie heute so viel produziert, so geschieht das hauptsächlich um der Investitionen willen. Die Industrie bedient keine Grundbedürfnisse, sondern fabriziert Wiederholungen, modische Abänderungen oder Erzeugnisse, die sich als absatzfähig erwiesen haben. Architekten und Zeichner sind ihre ahnungslosen Komplizen.

Via Apea

Der Mensch ist ein akrobatisches Tier, dem es schließlich gelungen ist, auf seinen Hinterbeinen zu stehen, aber sein Geist kriecht noch immer auf allen Vieren. Er sollte wissen, dass alle Erfindungen, die er durch seinen Intellekt erzielt, schon lange zuvor von Poeten ersonnen wurden. Um das zu beweisen, muss man nicht erst an die Ideen eines Leonardo da Vinci oder die Schriften eines Cyrano de Bergerac (der 1640 den Fonografen beschrieb) erinnern. Die Dichtung zeugt seit den frühesten Zeiten davon.

Die Misere des Menschen liegt weit tiefer: in seiner Unfähigkeit, etwas zu bauen, das nicht der Fantasie entsprungen ist.
Er ist ganz und gar gefangen im Netz seiner Vorstellungskraft.
Die Natur hält ihn in Geiselhaft.
Könnte er dieses Netz zerreißen – wäre er frei.
Doch der Mensch wandelt auf der Via Ape (Straße der Nachäffung). Es ist sein Schicksal nachzuäffen.
Im besten Fall, sich selbst nachzuäffen. Seine eigenen Visionen mechanisch zu verwirklichen.

24 ARCHITECTURAL STUDY, AROUND 1950
ARCHITEKTURSTUDIE, UM 1950

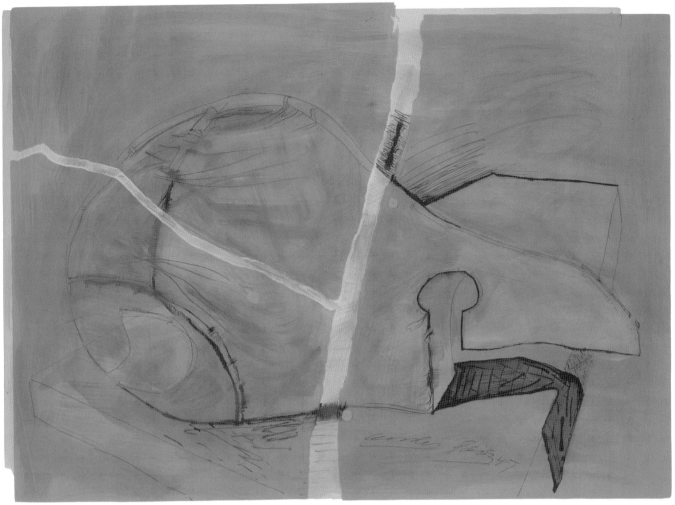

24

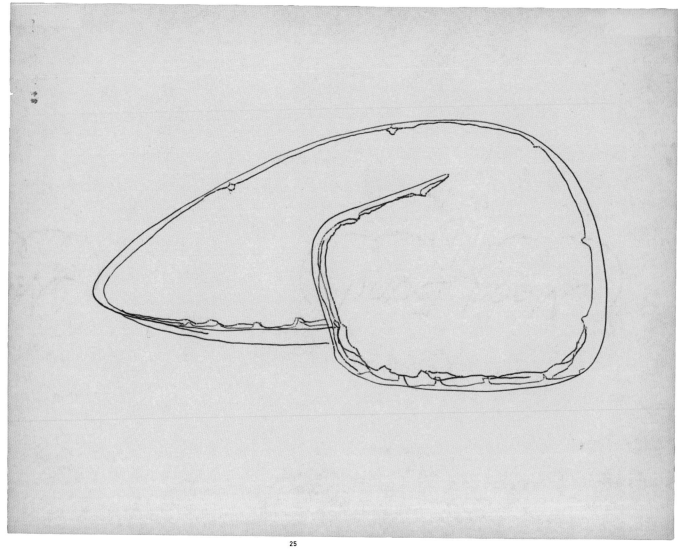

25-26 STUDIE FÜR EIN *TOOTH HOUSE*, UM 1950

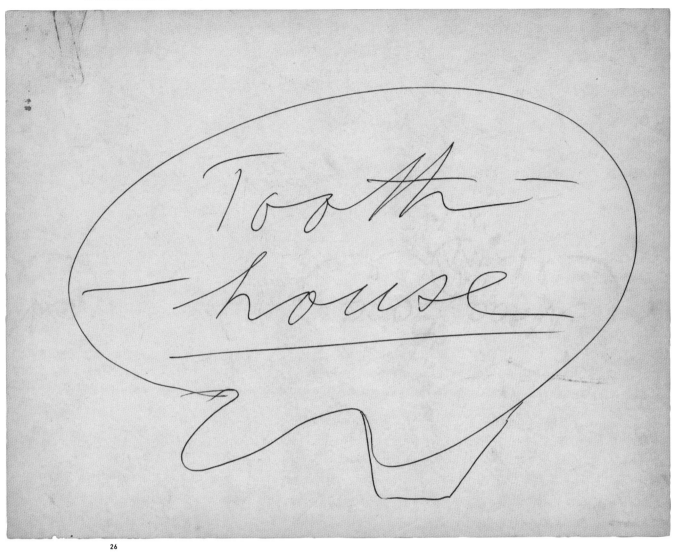

26

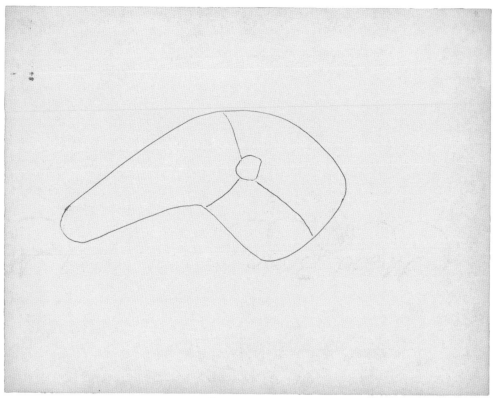

27

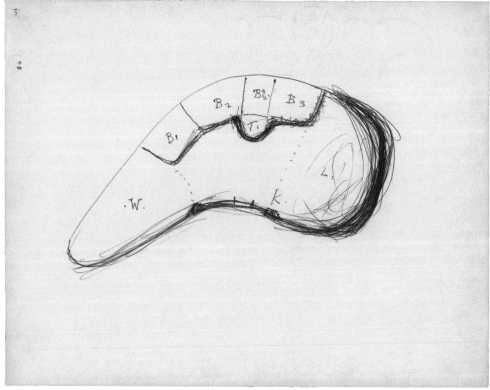

28

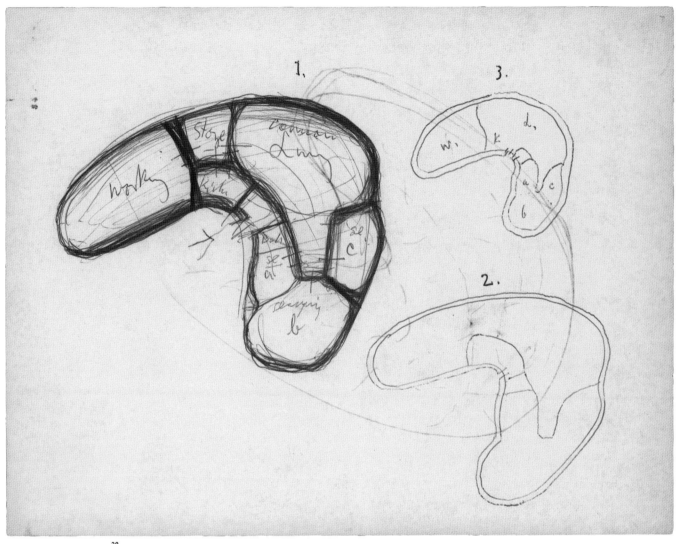

29

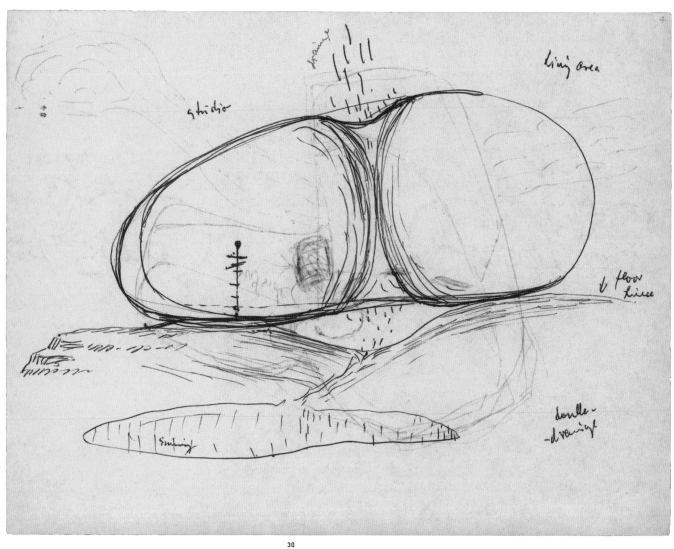

30–31 STUDIE FÜR EIN *TOOTH HOUSE*, UM 1950

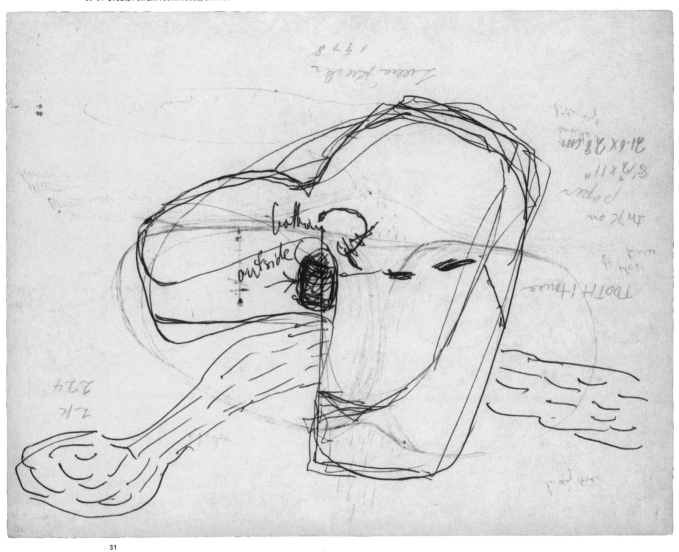

31

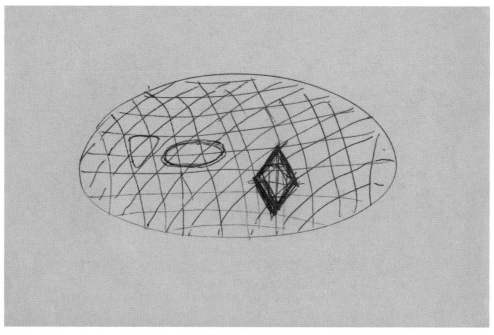

32

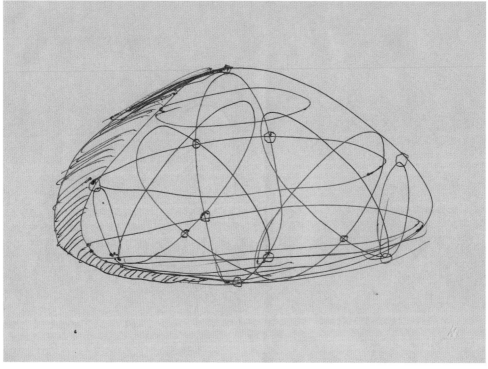

33

32–35 STUDIE FÜR EIN *ENDLESS HOUSE*, UM 1950

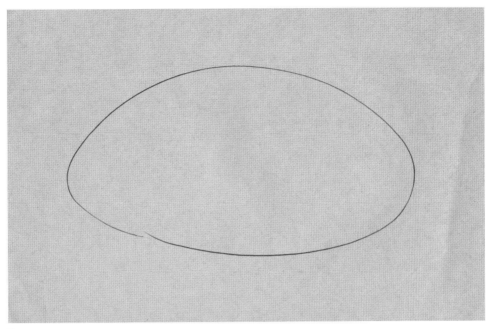

34

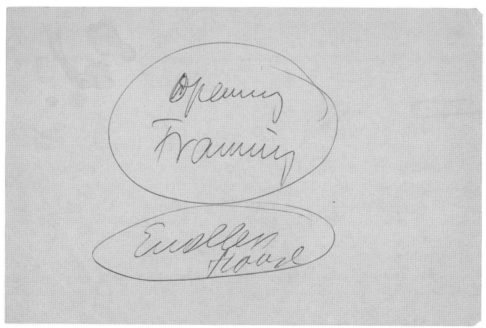

35

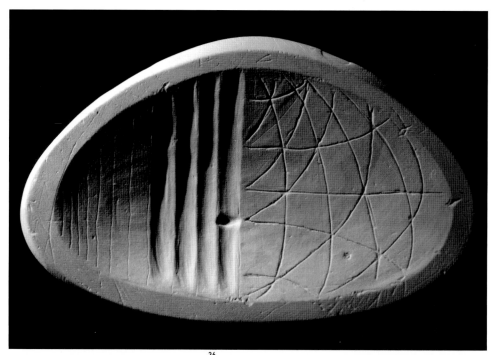

36

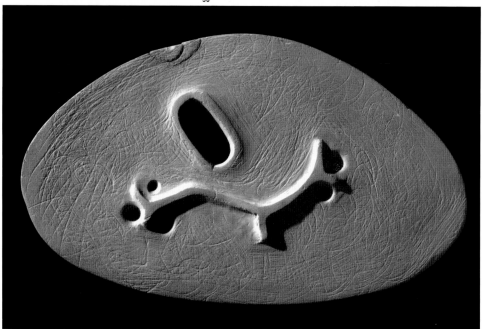

37

36–38 MODELL *ENDLESS HOUSE* FÜR DIE KOOTZ GALLERY, 1950

38

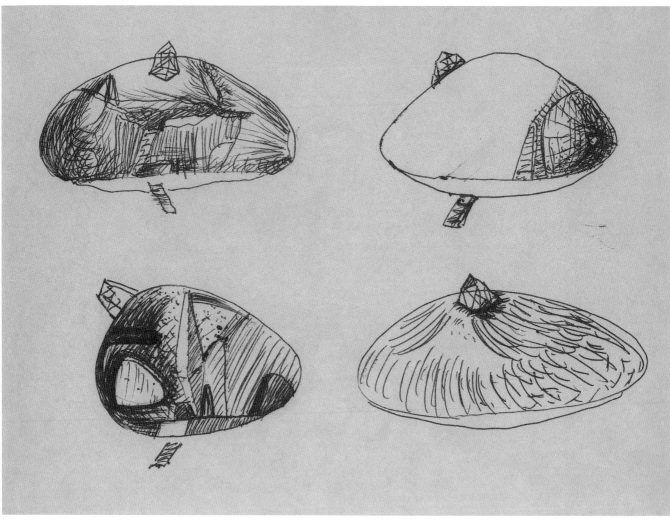

39 STUDIE FÜR EIN *ENDLESS HOUSE*, UM 1950
40 MODELL *ENDLESS HOUSE* FÜR DIE KOOTZ GALLERY, 1950

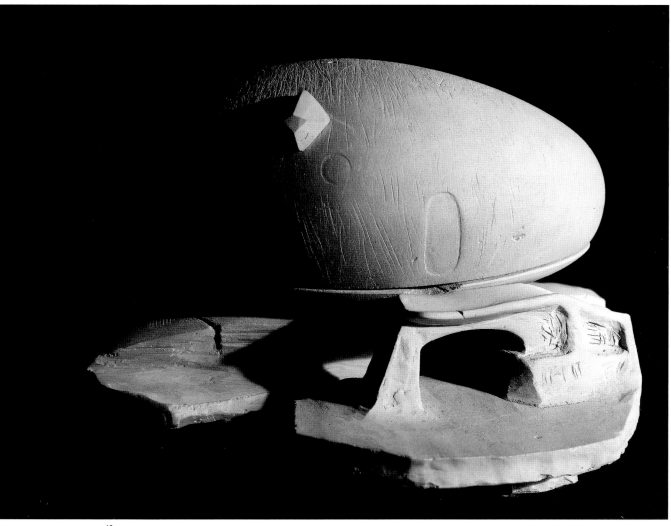

40

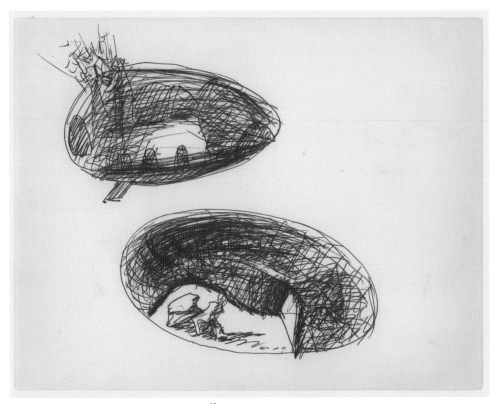

41

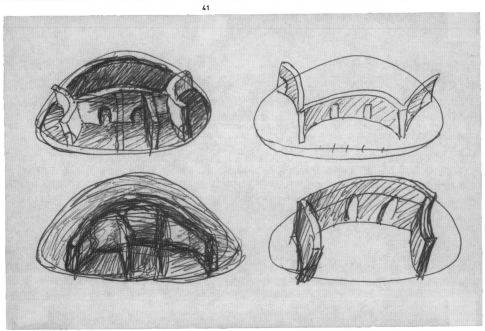

42

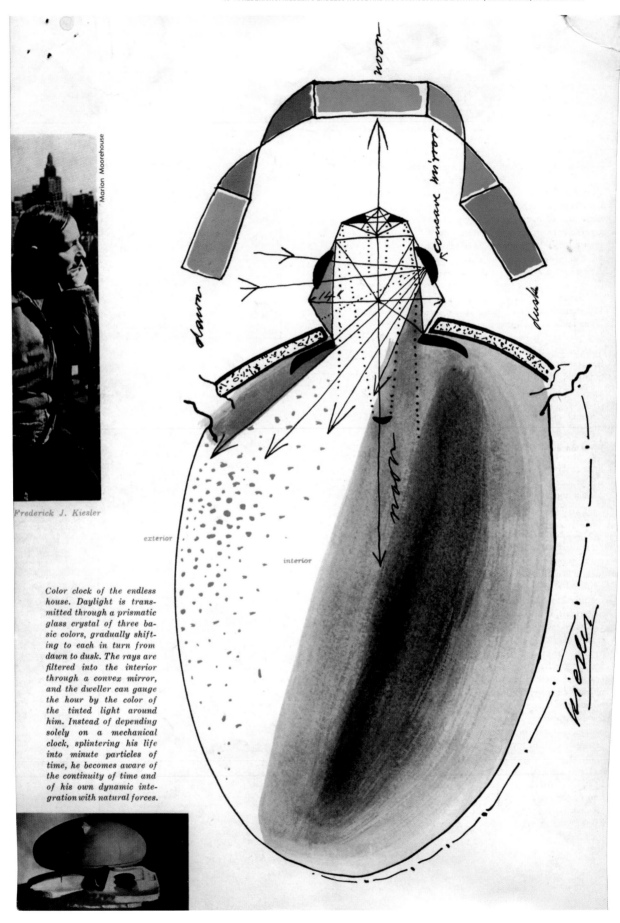

Marion Moorehouse

Frederick J. Kiesler

Color clock of the endless house. Daylight is transmitted through a prismatic glass crystal of three basic colors, gradually shifting to each in turn from dawn to dusk. The rays are filtered into the interior through a convex mirror, and the dweller can gauge the hour by the color of the tinted light around him. Instead of depending solely on a mechanical clock, splintering his life into minute particles of time, he becomes aware of the continuity of time and of his own dynamic integration with natural forces.

Frederick J. Kiesler's
endless house
and its psychological lighting

The endless house is an architectural form based on a lighting system designed to do more than merely give physical information. Primordial man had to kindle a twig and carry it to the shadowy corner of his cave in order to make out what was in the darkness. By now technical achievements have given us the power to use light—both natural and

windows

Rainford

artificial—to do more than serve our practical seeing needs. Light can push back the physical boundaries of our homes and surround us with stimulating color and exuberating brilliance; or it can set us apart in sharply defined work spaces in which to study, read, concentrate; or it can cradle us securely in remote havens of rest. Technically, all the functions that lighting can perform in a house boil down to general lighting

and spot lighting, and the problems involved can be classified as (a) installation, (b) operation and (c) maintenance. The endless house is more economical to light than a conventional building because its volume is not boxed into rooms. Uninterrupted, overflowing, reflected on curving surfaces, the light multiplies itself, and even the minimal amount switched on only to enable us to see gives us physical information over a wider area.

The continuous, flowing, shell construction of the endless house is not a fancy sculptural idea nor is it the imitation of an egg. The spheroid shape derives from the social dynamics of two or three generations living under one roof. The

upper entrance

view window

group living

ramp

eating

up

fireplace

kitchen

daylight

down

sound-proof study

children's playground
and
workshop

daylight

individual recreation
and sleeping

individual recreation
and sleeping

individual recreation
and sleeping

daylight

daylight

daylight

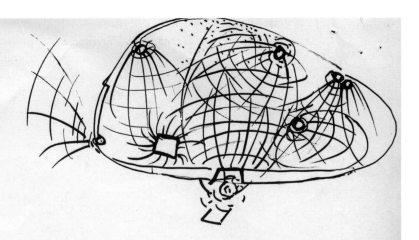

In addition to the sources of natural light—the many varied (in shape) windows that bring daylight into the shell, there is a strictly planned distribution of artificial light sources at every level of the shell, beaming light from the sides, ceiling, and floor.

generous spaces preferable for group living demand double or even triple heights in such areas as the living room, while minimal 8-foot heights are best in bedrooms and other private areas.

The curving shell of the house provides excellent vantage-points for carefully distributed, built-in filament and gaseous light sources, which send out vertical, diagonal, and horizontal beams adaptable to varied purposes. A beam shot from the ceiling to a whitish wooly carpet (a partly absorbing surface is better than a dazzling one), is bounced back to the ceiling and thence diffused over a wide area. The illustration below shows the very different effect obtained with a single direct beam shot

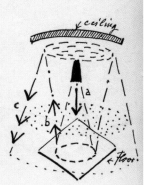

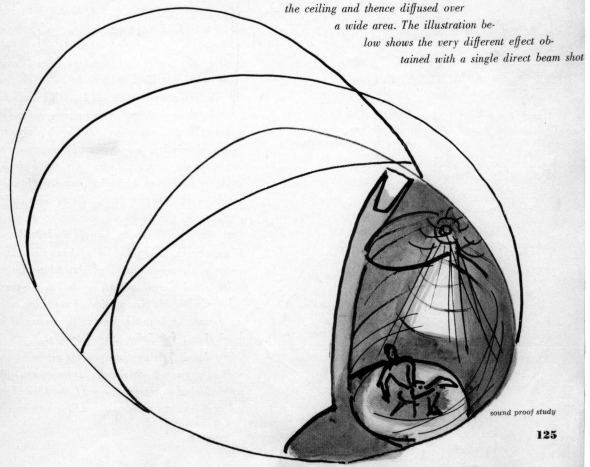

sound proof study

125

from the side at an angle. Whereas the double-direct-indirect lighting scheme just describ...
is exhilarating and appropriately gay for social gatherings, a single beam at the proper angle is more congenial for concentration and study.

Daylight raises different problems. We now have at our disposal three technical means of controlling daylight: (1) Dimensioning of the cut-outs—more commonly referred to as windows—through which daylight enters the building. We can make them large or small, round or rectangular. (2) Shielding the aperture or path of the light with a diffusing skin of glass, plastic, or a translucent woven material. (3) Masking the aperture with one of any number of disguises to temper or deflect the light —shades, louvers, and shutters.

The light source itself is usually ignored. We do not suggest an attempt to turn on the sun, but, although it has rarely been done by architects, it is possible to send sunlight through a lens in order to concentrate it, and pass it through convex mirror reflex devices to diffuse it. The color clock of the endless house illustrated on our introductory page is designed to do these things, as well as to fill the interior with color and make the dweller organically aware of the continuity of time.

At the top of this page we see the effect of tinting the interior of the house with the light filters of the color clock. The second drawing shows a completely different kind of daylight to be seen in the endless house—a direct beam of sunshine breaking through the six-foot circular opening—or call it a round window—in the children's playroom. The third drawing, a night view of the entrance as one opens the door, illustrates the psychologically evocative quality of the endless house. Light coming in parallel to the floor spills to the curving partitions of the interior, transforming it into a vast succession of shadows beyond shadows.

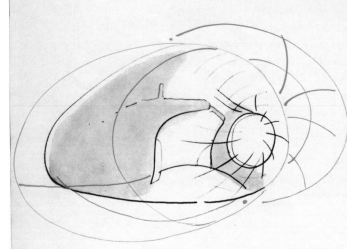

The apertures cut into the shell of the endless house —the windows—admit more light and for longer daily periods than if this curving shell were a vertical plane. The big view window of the living room reverses its angle to the floor in the course of its gradual curve, and also curves laterally.

The colored lines on the drawings represent (as well as any two dimensional illustration can) the psychological awareness of space beyond the physical partitions and walls of the endless house which

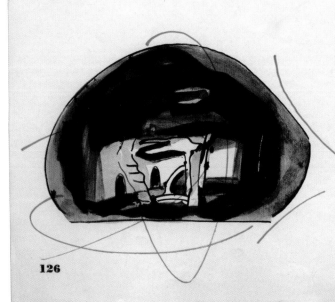

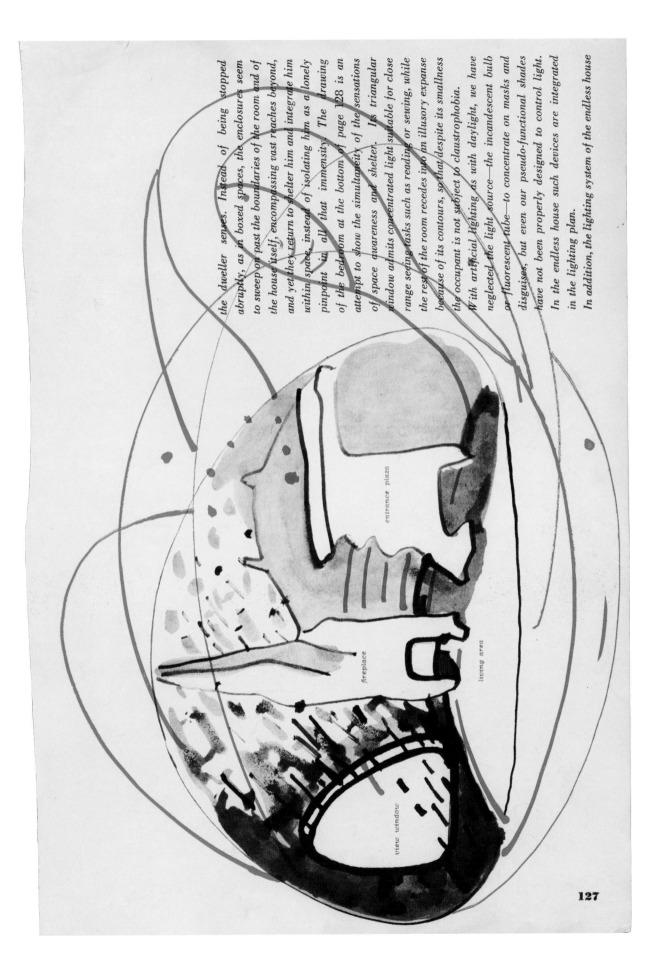

the dweller senses. Instead of being stopped abruptly, as in boxed spaces, the enclosures seem to sweep on past the boundaries of the room and of the house itself, encompassing vast reaches beyond, and yet they return to shelter him and integrate him within space, instead of isolating him as a lonely pinpoint in all that immensity. The drawing of the bedroom at the bottom of page 128 is an attempt to show the simultaneity of the sensations of space awareness and shelter. Its triangular window admits concentrated light suitable for close range seeing tasks such as reading or sewing, while the rest of the room recedes into an illusory expanse because of its contours, so that despite its smallness the occupant is not subject to claustrophobia.

With artificial lighting as with daylight, we have neglected the light source—the incandescent bulb or fluorescent tube—to concentrate on masks and disguises, but even our pseudo-functional shades have not been properly designed to control light. In the endless house such devices are integrated in the lighting plan.

In addition, the lighting system of the endless house

entrance plaza

fireplace

living area

view window

127

includes 1. Traveling light sources (*on trolleys*) *to get light exactly where it is wanted with relatively few sources.* 2. *Elastic light, rheostatically controlled dimmers raising and lowering the wattage at the dweller's will.* 3. *A system of electric eyes to turn lights on automatically. Connected to the rheostats, they would enable light to accompany the dweller wherever he walks in the house, and to brighten, or dim and disappear depending on whether he stays or goes on. If these were geared to a color control system one can easily surmise the tremendous range of visual stimulation available to the dweller's*

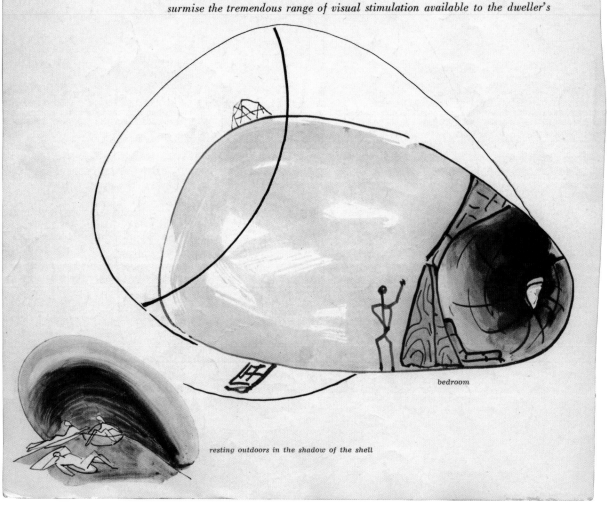

bedroom

resting outdoors in the shadow of the shell

Exterior at night, with both upper and lower entrances illuminated.

imagination. However fantastic such projects sound from a practical standpoint, let the reader rest assured that all necessary wiring, switching, and dimmer mechanisms are readily available on the market today. The lighting experts have simply failed to coordinate them properly in the home. I found no difficulty in obtaining them for my first attempt to develop such a lighting scheme, in Peggy Guggenheim's Gallery, "Art of This Century," seven years ago. The lighting system is quite feasible, and so is the endless house itself.—Frederick Kiesler

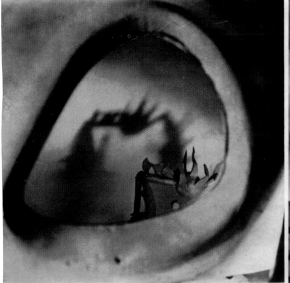

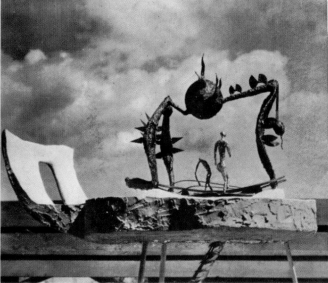

David Hare designed a huge sculpture which frames the head of the stairs leading from lower to upper level. At left is a view of it and its evocative shadows as seen from the living room window. At right, photo of the model taken with most of the house shell removed to get a full view of the sculpture. (The figures are not part of the composition, are included only to give the human scale.)

129

FREDERICK J. KIESLER'S ENDLESS HOUSE AND ITS PSYCHOLOGICAL LIGHTING[1]

Das *Endless House* ist eine architektonische Form, basierend auf einem Lichtsystem, das mehr kann, als nur physische Informationen zu geben. Der Mensch der Vorzeit musste einen Zweig entzünden und in die finsteren Ecken seiner Höhle tragen, um zu erkennen, was sich in der Dunkelheit verbarg. Heute ermöglicht uns der technische Fortschritt, Licht – natürliches und künstliches – umfassender einzusetzen als nur im Dienste unserer praktischen Sehbedürfnisse. Das Licht kann die physischen Grenzen unserer Häuser erweitern und uns mit anregenden Farben und erfrischender Strahlkraft umgeben; oder uns scharf abgezirkelte Arbeitsbereiche schaffen, in denen wir studieren, lesen, uns konzentrieren können; oder uns in abgeschiedenen Ruhezonen ein Gefühl der Sicherheit schenken. Technisch gesehen lassen sich alle möglichen Funktionen des Lichts in einem Haus zusammenfassen als allgemeine Beleuchtung und punktuelle Beleuchtung; die sich daraus ergebenden Probleme fallen in die Kategorien (a) Installation, (b) Betrieb und (c) Wartung. Das *Endless House* geht mit Licht ökonomischer um als ein konventionelles Gebäude, da sein Volumen nicht in Zimmer verschachtelt ist. Ununterbrochen, überfließend, sich auf gekurvten Oberflächen spiegelnd, multipliziert sich das Licht selbst, und sogar die minimale Lichtmenge, die bloß eingeschaltet wird, damit wir etwas sehen, vermittelt uns physische Informationen über einen größeren Bereich.

Die kontinuierliche, fließende Schalenkonstruktion des *Endless House* ist weder eine ausgefallene bildhauerische Idee noch die Imitation eines Eis. Die Kugelform ergibt sich aus der sozialen Dynamik, die entsteht, wenn zwei oder drei Generationen unter einem Dach leben. Die für das Zusammenleben in der Gruppe vorzuziehenden großzügigen Räume verlangen eine doppelte oder sogar dreifache Raumhöhe in Bereichen wie dem Wohnzimmer, während minimale Höhen von 2,5 Metern am besten für Schlafzimmer und andere private Bereiche geeignet sind.

Die gekurvte Schale des Hauses bietet ausgezeichnete Ansatzpunkte für gut verteilte, eingebaute Glühlampen und Leuchtstoffröhren, die vertikale, diagonale und horizontale Strahlen aussenden, die sich unterschiedlich nutzen lassen. Ein Lichtstrahl von der Decke auf einen weißlichen Wollteppich (eine teilweise absorbierende Oberfläche ist besser als eine glänzende) wird an die Decke zurückgeworfen und von dort über einen weiten Bereich gestreut. Die Illustration unten (siehe Seite 53 unten) zeigt die ganz spezielle Wir-

kung, die man mit einem einzelnen Lichtstrahl von der Seite in einem bestimmten Winkel erzielt. Während das soeben beschriebene doppelte direkt-indirekte Beleuchtungsschema belebend und fröhlich genug für gesellige Anlässe ist, eignet sich ein einzelner Lichtstrahl im richtigen Winkel eher für Konzentration und Studium.

Das Tageslicht wirft andere Probleme auf. Wir verfügen derzeit über drei technische Möglichkeiten, das Tageslicht zu kontrollieren: (1) Die Dimensionierung der Ausschnitte – allgemeiner Fenster genannt –, durch die das Tageslicht ins Gebäude dringt. Wir können sie groß oder klein, rund oder rechteckig gestalten. (2) Die Abschirmung der Öffnung oder des Lichtweges mittels einer diffundierenden Haut aus Glas, Plastik oder einem lichtdurchlässigen, gewebten Material. (3) Die Abdeckung der Öffnung mit einer beliebigen Verhüllung, um das Licht zu mildern oder abzulenken – Rollos, Jalousien und Fensterläden.

Die Lichtquelle selbst wird üblicherweise ignoriert. Wir regen nicht zum Versuch an, die Sonne einzuschalten, doch - obwohl Architekten es selten tun - ist es möglich, Sonnenlicht durch eine Linse zu leiten, um es zu bündeln und es dann durch eine reflektierende Konvexspiegel-Vorrichtung zu schicken, um es zu streuen. Die auf der ersten Seite abgebildete Farbuhr des *Endless House* (siehe Seite 50 rechts) wurde eigens für all diese Zwecke entworfen, erfüllt zudem den Innenraum mit Farbe und führt dem Bewohner die Kontinuität der Zeit vor Augen.

Oben auf dieser Seite (siehe Seite 54 oben) sehen wir den Effekt der Tönung des Hausinnenraums durch die Lichtfilter der Farbuhr. Die zweite Zeichnung (siehe Seite 54 mitte) zeigt eine völlig andere Art von Tageslicht, die man im *Endless House* erleben kann: einen direkten Sonnenstrahl, der durch die zwei Meter große kreisförmige Öffnung – man kann sie auch als rundes Fenster bezeichnen – ins Spielzimmer der Kinder fällt. Die dritte Zeichnung (siehe Seite 54 unten), eine Nachtansicht des Eingangsbereichs bei geöffneter Tür, veranschaulicht den psychologischen Beziehungsreichtum des *Endless House*. Parallel zum Boden hereinfallendes Licht ergießt sich bis zu den gekurvten Unterteilungen des Innenraums und verwandelt ihn in eine ausgedehnte Abfolge von Schatten hinter Schatten.

Die in die gekurvte Schale des *Endless House* geschnittenen Öffnungen – die Fenster – lassen mehr und länger Licht herein, als es bei einer vertikalen Ebene der Fall wäre. Das große Panoramafenster des Wohnraums ändert seinen Win-

1 In: *Interiors*, November 1950

kel zum Boden im Verlauf seiner graduellen Krümmung und wölbt sich auch zu den Seiten hin.

Die farbigen Linien in den Zeichnungen stellen (so gut das eine zweidimensionale Illustration vermag) das psychologische Bewusstsein des Bewohners für den Raum jenseits der physischen Unterteilungen und Wände des *Endless House* dar. Anstatt abrupt zu enden wie verschachtelte Räume, scheinen die Wände über die Grenzen des Zimmers und des Hauses selbst hinauszuwachsen und weitläufige Bereiche zu umfangen; dennoch kehren sie zurück, um den Bewohner innerhalb des Raums schützend zu bergen und zu integrieren, statt ihn als einsamen Punkt in all dieser Unermesslichkeit zu isolieren. Die Zeichnung (siehe Seite 56 unten) des Schlafzimmers unten auf Seite 128 ist ein Versuch, die Gleichzeitigkeit der Eindrücke von Raumbewusstsein und Schutz darzustellen. Sein dreieckiges Fenster lässt gebündeltes Licht ein, das für nahe Tätigkeiten wie Lesen oder Nähen geeignet ist, während der Rest des Zimmers aufgrund seiner Konturen in vorgeblicher Weite verschwindet, sodass trotz der kleinen Größe der Bewohner nicht an Klaustrophobie leiden muss.

Beim künstlichen Licht wie beim Tageslicht wird üblicherweise nicht auf die Lichtquelle eingegangen – die grell leuchtende Glühbirne oder die Leuchtstoffröhre –, sondern das Hauptaugenmerk auf Masken und Verkleidungen gelegt, doch selbst unsere pseudofunktionellen Rollos sind nicht dahin gehend entworfen, dass sie das Licht ordentlich regulieren. Im *Endless House* sind derartige Vorrichtungen in den Beleuchtungsplan integriert.

Zusätzlich umfasst das Beleuchtungssystem des *Endless House* 1. wandernde Lichtquellen (auf elektrischen Rollen), um mit relativ wenigen Quellen das Licht dorthin zu bekommen, wo man es braucht, 2. veränderliches Licht, bei dem über Widerstandsregler kontrollierte Dimmer die Wattanzahl nach Belieben des Bewohners regulieren, 3. ein System elektrischer Augen, das die Lichter automatisch einschaltet. Mit Rheostaten verbunden, würden sie es dem Licht ermöglichen, den Bewohner auf seinen Wegen durch das Haus zu begleiten, heller oder schwächer zu werden und zu verlöschen, je nachdem, ob er verweilt oder weitergeht. Sind diese Lichter auch noch an ein Farbkontrollsystem gekoppelt, kann man sich die ungeheure visuelle Stimulierung der Vorstellungskraft des Bewohners vorstellen. So fantastisch derartige Projekte von einem praktischen Standpunkt aus klingen mögen, der Leser sei versichert, dass sämtliche Verdrahtungs-, Schalt- und Dimmer-Mechanismen heute überall erhältlich sind. Die Lichtspezialisten haben es einfach versäumt, sie ordentlich im Haus zu koordinieren. Ich hatte keinerlei Schwierigkeiten, sie vor sieben Jahren für meinen ersten Versuch der Umsetzung eines solchen Beleuchtungsschemas in Peggy Guggenheims *Art of This Century Gallery* zu erwerben. Das Lichtsystem ist durchaus machbar, wie auch das *Endless House* selbst.

44 FREDERICK KIESLER WITH THE MODEL FOR *ENDLESS HOUSE*, AROUND 1960
FRIEDRICH KIESLER MIT MODELL DES *ENDLESS HOUSE*, UM 1960

44

FREDERICK KIESLER: HAZARD AND THE ENDLESS HOUSE[1], 1959

How to begin, how to end the *Endless House* was not a problem of start and finish. The idea has developed over forty years and it nests deep and wide all-over in my body, grain, muscles, nerves; is it part of my bloodstream, memories – past (sic) of past-moments. It's now a matter of timing when to cut loose somewhere the elastic mesh and let it out, which is to let the sea become a river of fountains, depth-charges erupting.

Technicalities of building a major shell, its subshells, the digestive tract of the house, the mechanisms for the control of air, heat, water, preparing food and sleeping had been stored, filed, catalogued over the years as a continuous growth of seedlings. It's part of the internal combustion process of germination, but will exist for others only in material configuration. The idea is not primeval anymore, pure, abstract, it breathes a reality of her own, embodying greater virility than pseudo-realization via clients, contractor, building departments. Law and control are created within. It's its own dictator. A hard nucleus to crack from the outside.

Drafting is grafting vision on paper with lead, ink, or – or. Blindfolded skating rather than designing, significantly keen, directed by experience and will, and channeling one's feelings and thoughts, deliberately proud of pruning them to clarity and definition. Chance drawing and sculpting or painting is an ability to let go, to be entirely tool rather than a guide of tools.

It is to design with one's whole body and mind, never mind-ful of either. No, it is not sketching, the bastard version between chance and will. It is capturing vision not seen through kodachromes, paper-book transparencies or sparking it by elbow-rubbing with pro-colleagues and new-marauders.

To maintain the steady flow, to maintain the honesty of its message is a hell of a difficult task for the inceptor, designer-builder. It's not a painting you can do in a flash or a sky-scratcher built layer after layer. A building is not art, nor a shelter-hut. Architecture is to make the superfluous functional. It is to support a heightened state of being, not simply to suffice. It is to exuberate, to inspire, to link, to help to correlate the awareness of the now with time ever present. All religious buildings of our civilizations have done it, but they only helped to pacify the unknown gods in cathedrals, pagodas – an architecture for ages dedicated to death. Architecture of the house dedicated to life does not exist yet. The *Endless House* is a first attempt at it. It's a twister; it brings the sky down and the earth up.

Wie man das *Endless House* beginnt, wie man es vollendet, war nicht ein Problem von Anfang und Ende. Die Idee hat sich über vierzig Jahre hinweg entwickelt, sie sitzt tief und überall in meinem Körper, in jeder Faser, in meinen Muskeln, meinen Nerven; sie ist in meinem Blut, in meinen Gedanken – ist Teil vergangener Momente. Es ist jetzt eine Frage des richtigen Zeitpunkts, wann man das elastische Geflecht an irgendeiner Stelle löst und es freisetzt, also das Meer zu einem Strom von Quellen werden lässt, Wasserbomben, die explodieren.

Technische Einzelheiten für den Bau einer Hauptschale, ihrer Unterteilungen, des Verdauungstrakts des Hauses, der Mechanismen für die Kontrolle von Luft, Wärme, Wasser, Zubereitung der Mahlzeiten und Schlafen waren über die Jahre gespeichert, abgelegt, katalogisiert worden wie ständig wachsende Sämlinge. Dies ist Teil des inneren Verbrennungsprozesses des Keimens, doch wird für andere nur in materiellen Konfigurationen existieren. Die Idee ist nicht länger ursprünglich, rein, abstrakt, sie atmet ihre eigene Realität, verkörpert eine größere Kraft als die Pseudoverwirklichung über Klienten, Bauunternehmer, Bauämter. Gesetz und Kontrolle entstehen aus ihr selbst. Sie ist ihr eigener Diktator. Ein von außen hart zu knackender Nukleus.

Entwerfen bedeutet, eine Vision aufs Papier zu übertragen, mit Bleistift, Tinte oder – oder. Mit verbundenen Augen zu gleiten, statt zu entwerfen, begeistert, geleitet von Erfahrung und Willen, und die eigenen Gefühle und Gedanken zu kanalisieren, im stolzen Bewusstsein, sie zu Klarheit und Genauigkeit zurechtzustutzen. Zeichnen, Bildhauerei oder Malerei nach dem Zufallsprinzip heißt, loslassen zu können, ganz Werkzeug zu sein, statt das Werkzeug zu führen.

Es bedeutet, mit ganzem Körper und Geist zu entwerfen, und dabei an keinen der beiden zu denken. Nein, damit ist nicht das Skizzieren gemeint, diese Zwitterversion zwischen Zufall und Willen. Es ist das Einfangen einer Vision, die nicht inspiriert wurde durch Farbfotografien oder Lichtbilder oder das Ellbogenreiben mit Berufskollegen und Plünderern von Neuem.

Das ständige Fließen zu bewahren, die Ehrlichkeit seiner Botschaft zu bewahren ist eine verdammt schwere Aufgabe für den Beginnenden, den Entwerfer-Erbauer. Es ist kein Bild, das man in null Komma nichts malen kann oder ein Etage um Etage gebauter Wolkenkratzer. Ein Gebäude ist weder Kunst noch eine Schutzhütte. Architektur bedeutet, das Überflüssige funktional zu machen. Es bedeutet, einem erhöhten Seinszustand zu dienen und nicht bloß zu genügen. Es bedeutet überzuschäumen, zu begeistern, zu verbinden, zu helfen, das Gespür für das Jetzt mit der immer gegenwärtigen Zeit zu correlieren. Alle religiösen Bauten unserer Zivilisationen haben das getan, doch sie haben nur dazu beigetragen, die unbekannten Götter in Kathedralen und Pagoden zu beschwichtigen – eine seit Ewigkeiten dem Tod verpflichtete Architektur. Architektur für das dem Leben verpflichtete Haus gibt es noch nicht. Das *Endless House* ist ein erster dahin gehender Versuch. Es ist ein Tornado; es wirbelt den Himmel herunter und die Erde nach oben.

1   »Hazard and the Endless House«, in: *Art News*, November 7, 1960

1   »Hazard and the Endless House«, in: *Art News*, 7. November 1960

46–47 MODELL DES *ENDLESS HOUSE*, UM 1960

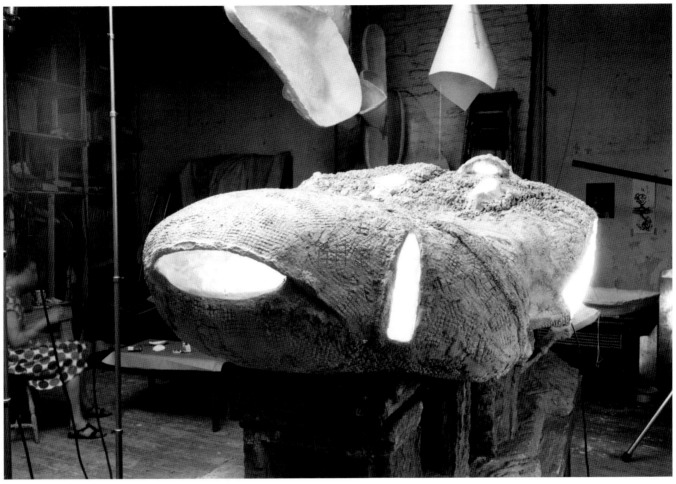

47

48 STUDIE ZU *ENDLESS HOUSE*, 1958-60
49 MODELL DES *ENDLESS HOUSE*, UM 1960

49

50–51 STUDIE FÜR *ENDLESS HOUSE*, 1958-60

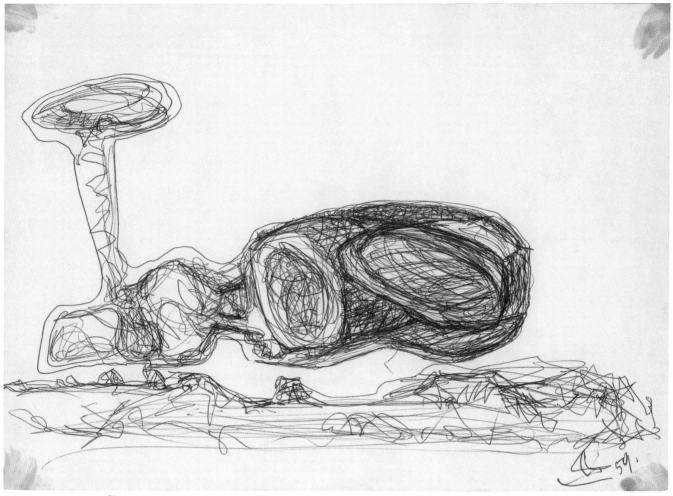

51

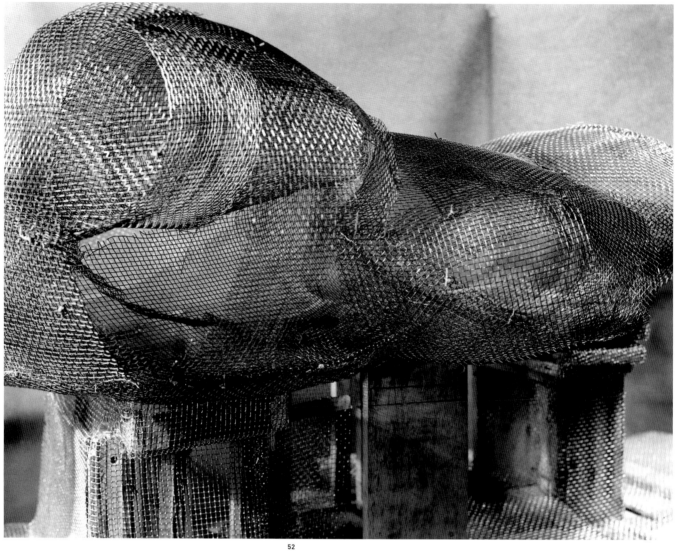

52–53 DRAHTSTRUKTUR ZUM MODELL DES *ENDLESS HOUSE*, UM 1959

53

54

54 MODELL DES *ENDLESS HOUSE* IN ARBEIT, UM 1959
55 STUDIE FÜR *ENDLESS HOUSE*, 1958-60

55

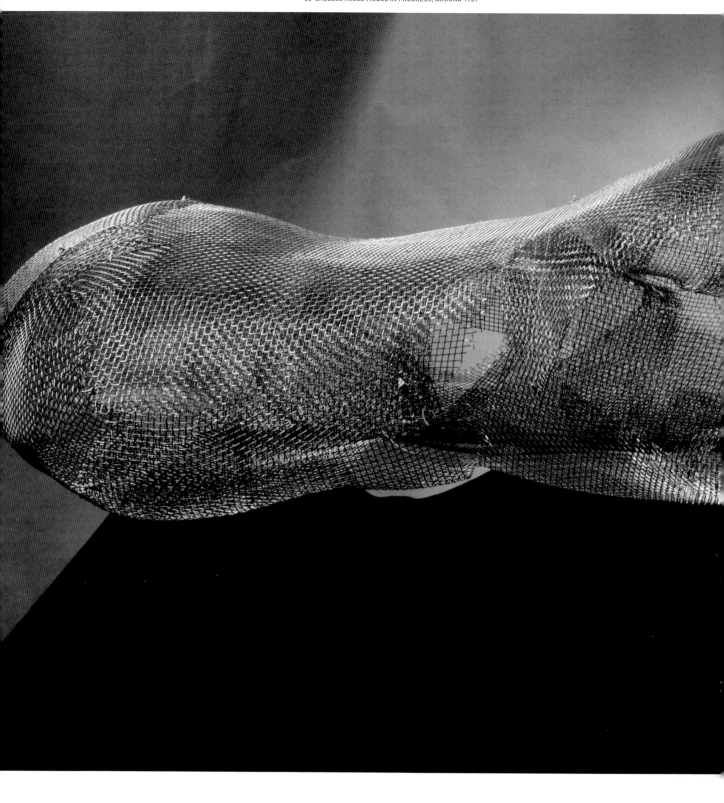

56

57–58 STUDIE ZU *ENDLESS HOUSE*, 1958-60

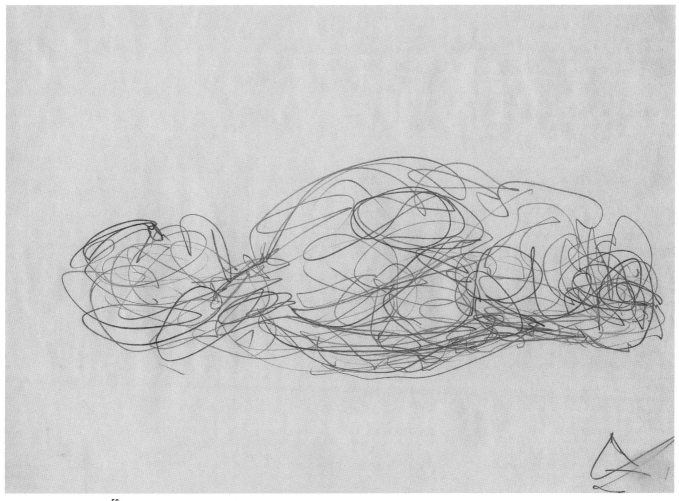

58

59 *WHEN I CONDUCT*, AROUND 1960

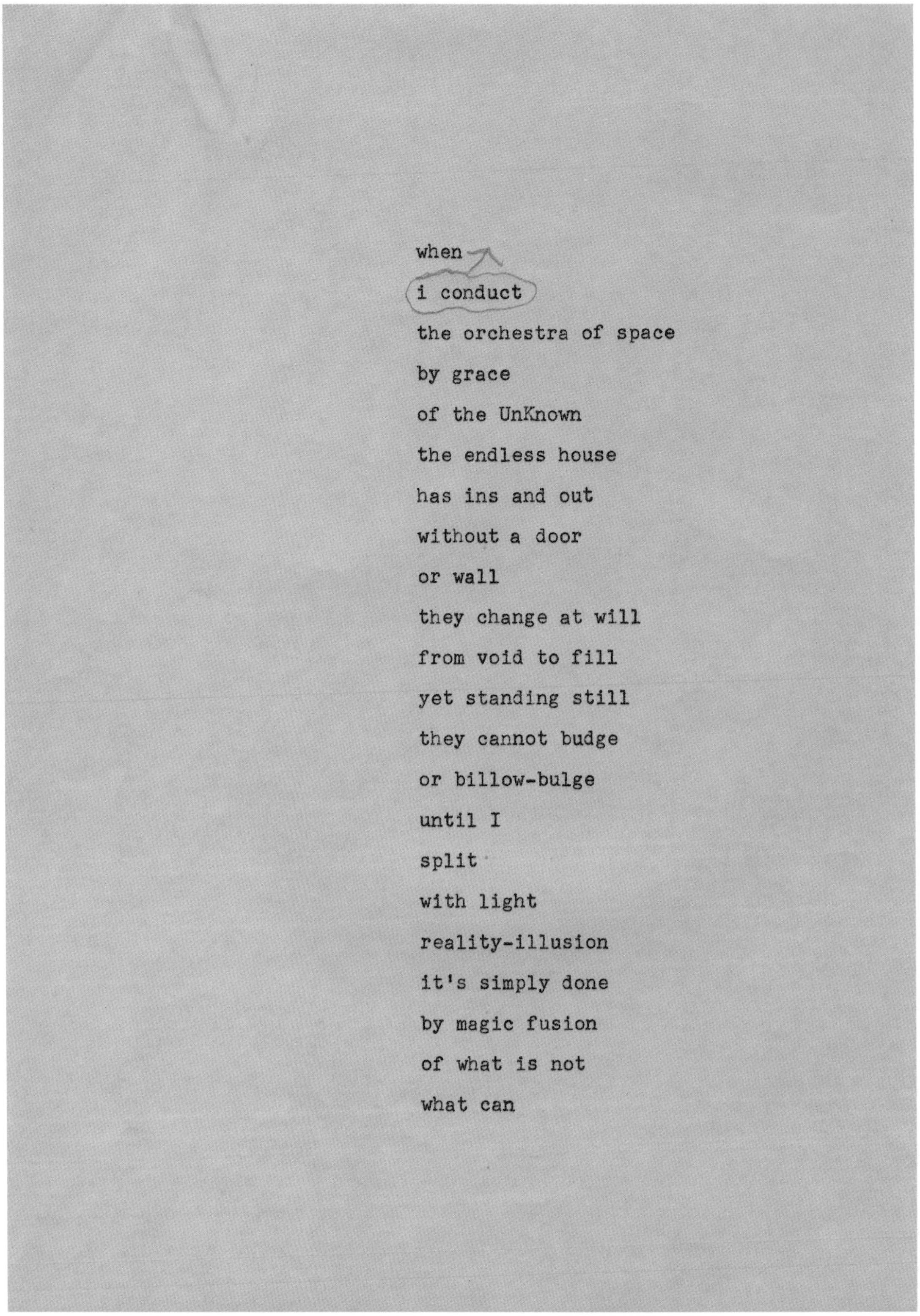

when
i conduct
the orchestra of space
by grace
of the UnKnown
the endless house
has ins and out
without a door
or wall
they change at will
from void to fill
yet standing still
they cannot budge
or billow-bulge
until I
split
with light
reality-illusion
it's simply done
by magic fusion
of what is not
what can

59 *WHEN I CONDUCT*, UM 1960

-2-

and does not want to be

yet must obey

oh! stay

succumb!

don't play me

dumb

my

scribble

nibbles

crumbs of mine

and Gods and Devils

fall

in line

59

  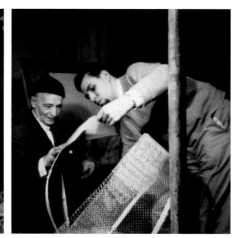

60–62

60–63 KIESLERS ATELIER MIT DEM MODELL DES *ENDLESS HOUSE* (KLEIN)
    IN ARBEIT, UM 1959

63

64–66

64–67 KIESLERS ATELIER MIT DEM MODELL DES *ENDLESS HOUSE* (SCHNITT)
IN ARBEIT, UM 1959

67

68 FREDERICK KIESLER'S INTERVIEW ON CBS, 1960
FRIEDRICH KIESLERS INTERVIEW FÜR CBS, 1960

FREDERICK KIESLER: *THE ENDLESS HOUSE* ON ›CAMERA THREE‹, CBS, 1960[1]

KIESLER The first idea comes to you simply like it is often said a dream, or an inspiration, or a vision. And then you are able to observe your life, the life of your co-human beings, and draw your conclusions. Living in boxes, no matter how many boxes you have – in a poor, in a richer, in the most luxurious house – they are still boxes and you feel encompassed by them, you feel hampered. You want to liberate yourself.

MacANDREW (...) Why is the house called the *Endless House*?

K Well, let me make you a very simple sign – you know the sign of infinity. Do you know that sign?

M Yes, indeed.

K Now see how it could be a two room *Endless House*, a two space *Endless House* or there is a continuity in a three room, three area unit – one, two, three. You see, we are now living in boxes, no matter how many boxes we are, we have or how many boxes constructed to make one apartment or one house, they are still very tight enclosures which cannot be moved, which cannot be opened up to our desires. The *Endless House* principle is a continuous flow of areas, of spaces. These areas, you see, are not of the same height or width as they are now, more or less, in houses which are one roof and floor above the other. They are exactly schemed to take care of our individual desires being absolutely alone, being together with somebody else, or finally opening up if we receive guests. Now this is the man's natural concept of houses. It means the end of the column and beam which is direct [sic] angle and which closes your area. (...)

M Now, we have here some simple models or elementary models, Mr. Kiesler, of the *Endless House*. Could you show them to us?

K Yes, I would gladly do so. Now this was the first stadium which lead finally to the *Endless House* (...) you see the main shell and then you see division within the main shell (...) the wall is curved and tried to relate the floor, ceiling, and the wall in a different way (...) in another model, which was made right afterwards (...) certain sections as you see are taken off so we can look better in. You see, take the two areas, which are called individual areas, are also a shell construction – one around the vertical axis and one around the horizontal axis. Can you see it? The house is also elevated from the floor, one floor up, that means that the cars drive underneath through. The one support is the staircase which leads up and you come into the middle of the living

KIESLER Die erste Idee kommt einem einfach, wie es so oft heißt, als Traum oder als Inspiration, als Vision. Und dann ist man in der Lage, sein eigenes Leben, das Leben seiner Mitmenschen zu betrachten und seine Schlüsse zu ziehen. In Schachteln zu wohnen, in wie vielen Schachteln auch immer – in einem armen, in einem reicheren, im luxuriösesten Haus –, es bleiben Schachteln, und man fühlt sich von ihnen umringt, fühlt sich eingeschlossen. Man möchte sich befreien.

MacANDREW (...) Warum heißt Ihr Haus *Endless House*?

K Erlauben Sie mir, dass ich Ihnen ein Zeichen skizziere – kennen Sie das Zeichen für Unendlichkeit? Kennen Sie dieses Zeichen?

M Ja, natürlich.

K Also sehen Sie, es könnte ein 2-Zimmer-*Endless-House* sein, ein Zweiraum-*Endless-House*, oder es gibt eine Kontinuität in einer Einheit mit drei Zimmern, drei Bereichen – eins, zwei, drei. Wir wohnen jetzt in Schachteln, egal, wie viele Schachteln wir haben oder wie viele Schachteln zu einer Wohnung oder einem Haus verbaut sind, sie bleiben enge Einfassungen, die nicht verschoben werden können, die sich nicht für unsere Wünsche öffnen lassen. Das Prinzip des *Endless House* ist ein kontinuierliches Fließen von Bereichen, von Räumen. Diese Bereiche haben nicht alle dieselbe Höhe oder Breite, wie es derzeit, mehr oder weniger, bei Häusern ist, die ein Dach und ein Stockwerk über dem anderen haben. Sie sind genau nach unseren individuellen Wünschen ausgerichtet, nämlich: allein zu sein, sich mit jemandem gemeinsam aufzuhalten oder aufzumachen, wenn wir Gäste empfangen. Das ist die natürliche Vorstellung des Menschen von einem Haus. Es bedeutet das Ende von Pfeiler und Balken, vom rechten Winkel, die den Wohnbereich eingrenzen. (...)

M Mr. Kiesler, wir haben hier ein paar einfache oder frühe Modelle des *Endless House*. Könnten Sie sie uns vorführen?

K Mit dem größten Vergnügen. Also das hier war das erste Stadium, das schließlich zum *Endless House* führte (...) Sie sehen die Hauptschale und dann die Unterteilung innerhalb dieser Schale (...) die Mauer ist gebogen und versucht, Boden, Decke und Wand auf neuartige Weise zu verbinden. (...) Im anderen Modell, das unmittelbar später entstand (...) wurden, wie Sie sehen, bestimmte Teile weggenommen, damit wir besser hineinschauen können. Sie sehen, die zwei Bereiche, die so genannten Individualbereiche, sind ebenfalls Schalenkonstruktionen – eine um die vertikale Achse und eine um die horizontale Achse. Können Sie es sehen? Das

1 The following interview has been edited from a transcription preserved in the archive of the Frederick Kiesler Center in Vienna. No changes have been made to this text except the cuts marked with (...). No grammatical or syntactical mistakes have been corrected in the English original version to maintain a spontaneous flow of thoughts as in the recorded version.
1 Das Interview wurde anhand eines Transkripts aus dem Archiv des Friedrich Kiesler-Zentrums in Wien bearbeitet. Im Text wurden Auslassungen mittels (...) gekennzeichnet. Grammatikalische oder syntaktische Fehler in der englischen Originalversion wurden belassen, in der Übersetzung jedoch dem heutigen schriftsprachlichen Gebrauch angepasst.

room out, which is a double height room and which gives you all the width which is necessary for a big expanse.

M Would these foundation units be a typical feature of the *Endless House*?

K I personally prefer it but it can just as well be on the ground or could be floating on the water or on sand. It is reinforced concrete and it is tight, airtight, and can do almost anything and is independent of deep foundations.

M (...) There was an editorial just recently that we came across in *Art News* which emphasizes the point – the relationship between the sculptor and the architect. (...) This editorial says in part »creative artists have, as long ago as the 1930s, moved from the classicism of geometric space to the organic surges of free form (...) Wright's Guggenheim Museum and Dallas Theatre, Le Corbusier's chapel at Ron-

Haus ist zudem vom Boden abgehoben, auf die Höhe des ersten Stocks; das bedeutet, dass unten Autos durchfahren können. Die einzige Stütze ist die Treppe, die nach oben führt, mitten in den Wohnraum hinein, der ein Raum mit doppelter Höhe ist und einem all den Platz bietet, den man braucht, um sich auszubreiten.

M Sind diese Einheiten mit Fundament typisch für das *Endless House*?

K Ich persönlich ziehe sie vor, aber es [das *Endless House*] kann genauso gut ebenerdig sein, es könnte auch auf dem Wasser oder auf Sand schweben. Es ist aus Stahlbeton und kompakt, luftdicht, es kann fast alles und braucht kein tiefes Fundament.

M (...) Wir sind auf einen kürzlich erschienenen Leitartikel in *Art News* gestoßen, der die Beziehung zwischen Bildhauer

 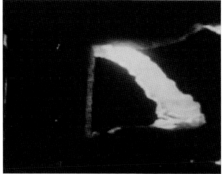 

champ and his Philips Electric Pavilion at the 1958 Brussel's Fair, Saarinen's TWA Terminal now being completed at Idlewild – each of these illustrating new possibilities of enclosed space bound to no corner or square. A culmination« – *Art News* goes on to say – »so far is Frederick Kiesler's concrete *Endless House*, building curled-up room enclosures together into a huge honeycomb.« Mr. Kiesler, can you tell us briefly how this all evolved.

K You ask really a lot because you know it is about ten centuries but let's try to put it in five minutes. (...) Let's start with the tree. Now a tree with all his branches, and his roots and here is the earth. You cut it up and you have a beam, a vertical beam, you take the same thing and try to put it horizontal to form a roof, but naturally you have to tie it here together so it is a problem of joints. You also have to support the other end, otherwise it is falling down, you know. Then you have to put it into foundation because it is insecure. (...) Now here you have a steel beam and you have the same thing here as you had it in wood. If you want a higher building, you simply add another steel beam above, (...) but you also very often go into basement and sub-basement, and then you have a terrific foundation for the whole thing to hold it up and in place. (...) But then you have the problem of filling the holes out, the holes vertically, the holes horizontally and so you have six or seven main contractors which range from concrete, to steel, to brick, to stone, to glass and so forth. We try to do it the other way and simplify the matter. We have a cave which man first saw for shelter which is flat on the ground and where he crawls in for protection. Later on we see he developed the igloo, which is pre-manufactured dome with the exception that the parts, the individual parts, are frozen together and are frozen to the ground. Now, in the *Endless House*, you see, there are all these handicaps of building in parts which have to be fitted together, are eliminated. As a matter of fact, the *Endless House* has

und Architekt zum Thema hat. (...) Darin steht unter anderem zu lesen, dass »kreative Künstler schon in den 30ern vom Klassizismus des geometrischen Raums zu den organischen Ausbrüchen der freien Form übergegangen sind«. (...) Wrights Guggenheim Museum und Dallas Theatre, Le Corbusiers Kapelle von Ronchamp und sein Philips Electric Pavilion bei der Weltausstellung in Brüssel 1958, Saarinens TWA Terminal, das derzeit in Idlewild fertig gestellt wird – all diese Beispiele veranschaulichen neue Möglichkeiten für umschlossenen Raum, der nicht zwangsweise Ecken oder Quadrate aufweisen muss. »Einen Höhepunkt«, so *Art News* weiter, »stellt bislang Friedrich Kieslers *Endless House* aus Beton dar, das zusammengerollte Raumbereiche zu einer riesigen Honigwabe verbaut.« Mr. Kiesler, können Sie uns kurz schildern, wie sich das alles entwickelt hat?

K Da fragen Sie wirklich viel, denn wissen Sie, das sind gleich zehn Jahrhunderte, aber versuchen wir es in fünf Minuten zu verpacken. (...) Fangen wir beim Baum an. Ein Baum mit all seinen Ästen und seinen Wurzeln, und hier ist die Erde. Sie schneiden ihn um und haben einen Balken, einen senkrechten Balken; Sie nehmen dasselbe Ding und versuchen es waagrecht zu legen, um ein Dach zu bilden, aber natürlich müssen Sie es hier zusammenbinden, es gibt also ein Verbindungsproblem. Sie müssen auch das andere Ende abstützen, sonst fällt es herunter, verstehen Sie. Dann brauchen Sie ein Fundament, weil es instabil ist. (...) Hier haben Sie nun einen Stahlbalken, und es ist dasselbe wie in Holz. Wenn Sie ein höheres Gebäude wollen, fügen Sie einfach oben einen weiteren Stahlbalken an, (...) aber sehr oft bauen Sie auch nach unten in den Keller, und dann haben Sie ein wunderbares Fundament für das ganze Ding, das es aufrecht und an Ort und Stelle hält. (...) Doch dann stellt sich das Problem, dass Sie die Löcher ausfüllen müssen, die Löcher vertikal und die Löcher horizontal, und auf einmal haben Sie sechs oder sieben Zulieferanten von Beton, Stahl, Ziegeln,

not a single joint no matter how big it is. It is a continuous tension construction, different from what you see and from post and lintel as you know it. Now it is rather simple, the whole concept really is nothing very inventive, and nothing extraordinary. But you start, you see, you have domes before as you know with brick constructions. In order to hold the whole thing together you have to put it on the colonnade all around and then you have to put the colonnade into the ground again. (...) Today we can do it differently. We have reinforced concrete. We don't need any columns; we don't need any beams. We just continue the shell from the floor up into the wall, into the ceiling, and back into the wall. That doesn't mean that the house has to look like an egg – it can have any shape and form as long as the floor, sides, ceilings are superordinated, that they form an integrated unit which is

Stein, Glas und so weiter. Versuchen wir es jetzt andersrum und vereinfachen die Sache. Wir haben eine Höhle, die dem Menschen als erste Behausung diente, die flach auf dem Boden liegt und in die er kriecht, um Schutz zu finden. Später entwickelte er den Iglu, der eine vorgefertigte Kuppel ist, bloß dass die Teile, die einzelnen Teile, untereinander und mit dem Boden zusammengefroren sind. Im *Endless House* sind all diese Nachteile des Bauens in Teilen, die aneinander gefügt werden müssen, eliminiert. Tatsächlich hat das *Endless House* nicht eine einzige Verbindungsstelle, egal wie groß es ist. Es ist eine Konstruktion in kontinuierlicher Spannung, im Unterschied zu Pfeiler und Balken, wie man sie kennt. Es ist recht einfach; das ganze Konzept ist wirklich nicht besonders originell, nichts Außergewöhnliches. Nehmen Sie eine Kuppel, wie Sie sie kennen, wie bei einer Zie-

independent of digging it into the ground to just need a launching pad for it. That's all. Now the structure is then here heavy on the floor, goes thinner on the ceiling – should be here eleven inches and goes here to three and a half inches. That is the main structure of the *Endless House*. (...)

M Now most of us have had a look, whether we've understood it or not, of architect's plans. Now we have one of two plans of the *Endless House* here. Would you let us have a look at them?

K Gladly. Now this is the south view of the *Endless House* with the master unit right in front and you see a horizontal opening which is very large which you normally would call a window, which we call, you see, a fusion light unit, and then a vertical one on the left side, you see an exit stair. (...) And that of course is the view of the north side with what is called the dining and kitchen area. The big stretch in the middle is the living room area including the children quarters to the left. (...)

M How about some of the very ordinary areas in the average 20th century home, something like the bathroom, for instance.

K Well, that is a very complicated situation. It is just compose, you know, as a repetition of the same bowls in wood, then in enamel, in tin and now it might be in plastics, illuminated from below. But, you see, it is not the matter to enjoy the bathing because it gets cold, the heat cannot be regulated, etc. That can be very easily be taken care of.

M This calls for the same sort of fresh, breaking through of thinking as you've done before.

K Observation of the life processes and nothing else. But one of the main questions is, naturally, which I'm always asked, are the expenses of the thing. Now, I would like to say that a present estimate is (...) between 25 percent and 30 percent less expensive than even the same cubic content in brick.

gelkonstruktion. Um das ganze Ding zusammenzuhalten, müssen Sie eine Kolonnade rundherum bauen, und dann müssen Sie die Kolonnade wieder auf ein Fundament setzen. (...) Heute können wir das anders machen. Wir haben Stahlbeton. Wir brauchen keine Säulen, wir brauchen keine Balken. Wir lassen einfach die Schale vom Boden in die Wand, in die Decke und zurück in die Wand übergehen. Das bedeutet nicht, dass das Haus wie ein Ei aussehen muss – es kann jede Gestalt und Form haben, solange Boden, Seiten und Decken eine geschlossene Einheit bilden, die nicht im Boden verankert werden muss, bloß weil man eine Abschussrampe [als Verankerung] braucht. Das ist alles. Die Konstruktion ist hier am Boden massiv und wird an der Decke dünner – hier sollte sie 28 Zentimeter haben und hier neun. Das ist der grundsätzliche Aufbau des *Endless House*. (...)

M Die meisten von uns haben schon einmal, ob wir nun etwas damit anfangen konnten oder nicht, einen Blick auf die Pläne von Architekten geworfen. Hier haben wir nun einen von zwei Plänen des *Endless House*. Würden Sie sie uns zeigen?

K Gerne. Also das ist die Südansicht des *Endless House* mit dem Hauptbereich hier vorne, und Sie sehen eine waagrechte Öffnung, die sehr groß ist und die man normalerweise als Fenster bezeichnen würde, die wir jedoch *fusion light unit* [Verbindung aus künstlichem und natürlichem Licht] nennen, und dann eine senkrechte auf der linken Seite, sehen Sie, eine Treppe. (...) Und das ist natürlich die Nordansicht mit dem so genannten Ess- und Küchenbereich. Der große Teil in der Mitte ist der Wohnraum, der den Kinderbereich linker Hand mit einschließt. (...)

M Wie sieht es mit der Standardausstattung des Durchschnittsheims des 20. Jahrhunderts aus, dem Badezimmer zum Beispiel?

K Nun, das ist eine sehr komplizierte Angelegenheit. Beim Bad wurden bloß immer dieselben Wannen abgewandelt, in

M To what extent will the *Endless House* have individuality or will they all tend to sort of look alike?

K Not at all. You know, when I first started and you saw the first model, everybody thought that the *Endless House* will have to look like an egg, a squared-off egg. But as you have seen it, it isn't at all. (...) It depends on the location, it depends on the desire and size of the family, on the amount of money available and it should not be difficult for any imaginative designer to adopt that with an infinite variety.

M Mr. Kiesler, I'd like to thank you for being with us on behalf of »Camera Three« and on behalf of our viewers and I'd like to close by repeating very briefly something that Mr. Kiesler said. He said: »Technological environment is produced by human needs. Investigation of this crucial point cannot be based on a study of architecture but must be based

Holz, später dann in Email, in Blech, und jetzt vielleicht in Plastik mit Beleuchtung von unten. Aber sehen Sie, es ging nie darum, das Bad zu genießen, es kühlt aus, die Wärme kann nicht reguliert werden, etc. Das ist ganz leicht zu lösen.

M Das erfordert denselben unverbrauchten, bahnbrechenden Denkansatz wie schon zuvor.

K Beobachtung der Lebensprozesse und weiter nichts. Doch eine der häufigsten Fragen, die mir immer wieder gestellt wird, betrifft natürlich die Kosten. Ich möchte sagen, dass eine aktuelle Schätzung (...) zwischen 25 und 30 Prozent günstiger ausfällt als sogar bei einem Ziegelbau desselben Kubikinhalts.

M In welchem Ausmaß wird das *Endless House* individuell sein, oder werden alle eher gleich aussehen?

K Keineswegs. Wissen Sie, als ich damit begann und das

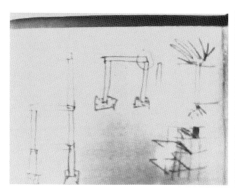
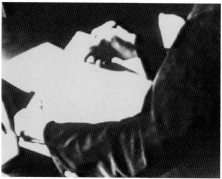

on a study of the life processes of man.« Now, if you have found [interesting] this discussion of the *Endless House* which was, by the way, the very first appearance of Mr. Kiesler's creation on television, why don't you send us your comment – just address them to »Camera Three«.

erste Modell fertig war, dachten alle, das *Endless House* würde wie ein Ei aussehen müssen, ein in Quadrate unterteiltes Ei. Aber wie Sie gesehen haben, ist das ganz und gar nicht der Fall. (...) Es hängt vom Baugelände ab, es hängt von den Wünschen und der Größe der Familie ab, vom zur Verfügung stehenden Geld, und es sollte für einen fantasievollen Designer kein Problem sein, unendlich viele Variationen davon zu entwerfen.

M Mr. Kiesler, ich möchte Ihnen im Namen von »Camera Three« und unseren Zuschauern für Ihr Kommen danken. Lassen Sie mich zum Abschluss noch ganz kurz etwas wiederholen, was Mr. Kiesler gesagt hat. Er sagte: »Das technologische Umfeld wird von menschlichen Bedürfnissen erzeugt. Eine Untersuchung dieses entscheidenden Punktes kann nicht auf einem Studium der Architektur beruhen, sondern muss auf einem Studium der Lebensabläufe des Menschen fußen.« Wenn diese Besprechung des *Endless House* – das hier übrigens zum ersten Mal im Fernsehen vorgestellt wurde – Ihr [Interesse] gefunden hat, schicken Sie uns doch Ihren Kommentar – richten Sie ihn einfach an »Camera Three«.

69 (FOLLOWING PAGE) INTERIOR VIEW OF
   THE *ENDLESS HOUSE* MODEL, AROUND 1960
   (NÄCHSTE SEITE) INNENSICHT DES MODELL DES *ENDLESS*
   HOUSE, **UM 1960**

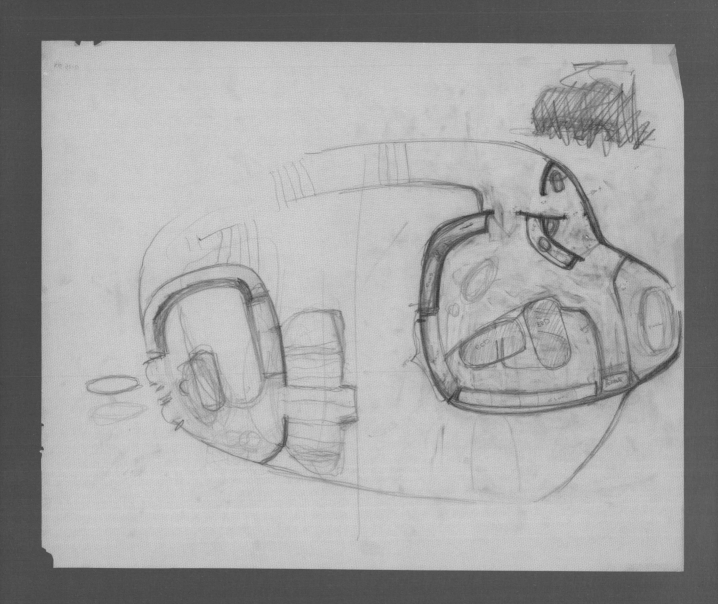

FREDERICK KIESLER: SHORT STATEMENTS ABOUT THE ENDLESS HOUSE, PERTAINING TO THE QUESTIONS USUALLY ASKED, 1961[1]

Form and Function

The form of the *Endless House* is not a free-flow art form, as many suspect, but derives from living a life which is simpler, and dedicated rather to fundamentals than to mechanized equipment and interior decoration. Thus, it tends definitely to assist in developing freer expression or fulfillment of the individual.

Even the window-areas are not standardized in size or shape, but are, rather, large and varied in their transparency and translucency and form part of the variety, however minute, of the concept of the house.

The measurement of the heights, widths and depths of the various areas for eating, resting, group-living or for seclusion, these individual architectural dimensions determine the form of the house. Every section of it can be closed off from the others, or, if necessary, be opened up, making one continuous area.

Construction

To achieve the desired results, a new construction principle had to be invented, which I called »continuous tension«, the material being concrete, in a great variety of textures and colors, outside and inside. This material may be easily molded, even without a form, and is less expensive than brick for a house of the same cubic content. Columns and beams are eliminated. The shell is waterproof and fireproof, and comparatively easy to maintain.

Floors

Floors are even; they only curve at the very edges, and differently in each area. As they continue up into walls and ceilings, they do not enclose the individual in strait-jackets of brick or glass, as any of the old or modern industrial walls do.

Furniture

It is advisable not to transfer old furniture into this house, since furniture is an integral part of the concept of the house. The furniture designed for it is of a more sculptural nature, in different materials, easily movable or built in.

Form und Funktion

Die Form des *Endless House* ist keine frei fließende Kunstform, wie viele annehmen, sondern leitet sich von einer einfacheren Lebensweise her und widmet sich mehr den Grundlagen als der mechanisierten Ausstattung und Innenraumgestaltung. Somit unterstützt sie definitiv die Entwicklung eines freieren Ausdrucks oder die Verwirklichung des Individuums. Selbst die Fensterbereiche sind nicht nach Größe oder Form genormt, sondern fallen eher groß aus, variieren in ihrer Durchsichtigkeit und Lichtdurchlässigkeit und zählen zu den – wenn auch minimalen – Variationsmöglichkeiten des Konzepts des Hauses.

Höhe, Breite und Tiefe der verschiedenen Bereiche für Essen, Erholung, Gemeinschaftsleben oder Zurückgezogenheit, diese individuellen architektonischen Dimensionen bestimmen die Form des Hauses. Jeder Abschnitt kann von den anderen abgeteilt oder, wenn nötig, zu ihnen hin geöffnet werden, um einen durchgehenden Bereich zu schaffen.

Bauweise

Um die gewünschten Resultate zu erzielen, musste ein neues Bauprinzip erfunden werden, das ich »kontinuierliche Spannung« genannt habe; sein Baustoff ist Beton in einer Vielzahl von Spielarten und Farben, für innen wie für außen. Dieses Material ist leicht formbar, auch ohne Schalung, und weniger kostspielig als Ziegel für ein Haus mit demselben Kubikinhalt. Säulen und Balken sind eliminiert. Die Schale ist wasserdicht, feuerfest und relativ leicht instand zu halten.

Böden

Die Böden sind eben; sie wölben sich nur an den Rändern, und das in jedem Bereich anders. Da sie in Wände und Decken übergehen, sperren sie das Individuum nicht in Zwangsjacken aus Ziegeln oder Glas, wie es alte oder die modernen vorgefertigten Wände tun.

Möbel

Es ist ratsam, keine alten Möbel in dieses Haus mitzunehmen, da das Mobiliar einen wichtigen Bestandteil des Hauskonzepts darstellt. Das eigens für dieses Haus entworfene Mobiliar ist mehr von bildhauerischer Natur, besteht aus verschiedenen Materialien und ist leicht beweglich oder fix eingebaut.

1 Unpublished typescript, undated, archive of the Kiesler Center, Vienna
1 Unveröffentlichtes Typoskript, undatiert, Archiv des Kiesler-Zentrums, Wien

Light

There are three kinds of lighting: a general lighting, indirect and smooth; direct lighting, coming through the openings in ceilings and sides during the day as well as at night; and small light-units, built in, which can be focused at any particular spot, as for reading, for example.

The effect of lighting is important in the *Endless* because it helps considerably to give to one and the same area the illusion of a more vast or more intimate space.

Closets

Storage space is provided by double shells along walls, especially in sleeping quarters, kitchen and dining areas.

Heating and Cooling

Heating is radiant, built into the floor. Natural or artificial control of temperature is optional.

Bath

There are no cut-off bathrooms; bathing, in the interior, forms part of an individual living quarter with the bed etc. As a matter of fact, each sleeping quarter is an individual living room.

Kitchen

The kitchen is part of the dining area, and connected with special storage space. Modern equipment can be installed, according to funds available.

Mechanized labor-saving devices

As for eating, cooking, cleaning, bathing, best modern equipment will be used whenever or wherever it is of great value to the household, but the design of any part of the house is not based on gadgets. It is based on simple, healthful and direct ways of living, where work is recreational activity, rather than drudgery.
While the concept of the house does not advocate »a return to nature«, it certainly does encourage a more natural way of living, and a greater independence from an automative way of life.

Licht

Es gibt drei Arten von Licht: eine allgemeine Beleuchtung, indirekt und weich; direktes Licht, das bei Tag wie bei Nacht durch die Öffnungen in den Decken und Seitenwänden fällt; und kleine, eingebaute Beleuchtungseinheiten, die auf eine bestimmte Stelle gerichtet werden können, etwa zum Lesen.

Der Effekt der Beleuchtung ist ein wesentlicher im *Endless* da sie beträchtlich dazu beiträgt, ein und denselben Bereich offener oder intimer wirken zu lassen.

Schränke

Stauraum wird durch doppelte Schalen entlang der Wände geboten, insbesondere in Schlafräumen, Küche und Essbereichen.

Heizung und Kühlung

Die Heizung arbeitet mit Strahlungswärme und ist in den Boden eingebaut. Eine natürliche oder künstliche Temperaturkontrolle ist frei wählbar.

Bad

Es gibt keine abgetrennten Badezimmer; das Bad, im Hausinneren, ist Teil eines individuellen Wohnbereichs mit dem Bett etc. Tatsächlich ist jeder Schlafbereich ein individueller Wohnraum.

Küche

Die Küche ist Teil des Essbereichs und mit einem speziellen Stauraum kombiniert. Moderne Ausstattung kann nach den verfügbaren Mitteln eingebaut werden.

Mechanisierte, Arbeit sparende Vorrichtungen

Für Essen, Kochen, Putzen und Baden wird die beste moderne Ausstattung verwendet, wann und wo immer sie dem Haushalt zugute kommt, doch das Design setzt nirgendwo im Haus auf bloße technische Spielereien. Es beruht auf einer einfachen, gesunden und direkten Lebensweise, bei der Arbeit eine erholsame Tätigkeit und nicht Plackerei darstellt.

Während das Konzept des Hauses nicht für ein »Zurück zur Natur« eintritt, unterstützt es zweifellos eine natürlichere Lebensweise und eine stärkere Unabhängigkeit von einem automatisierten Leben.

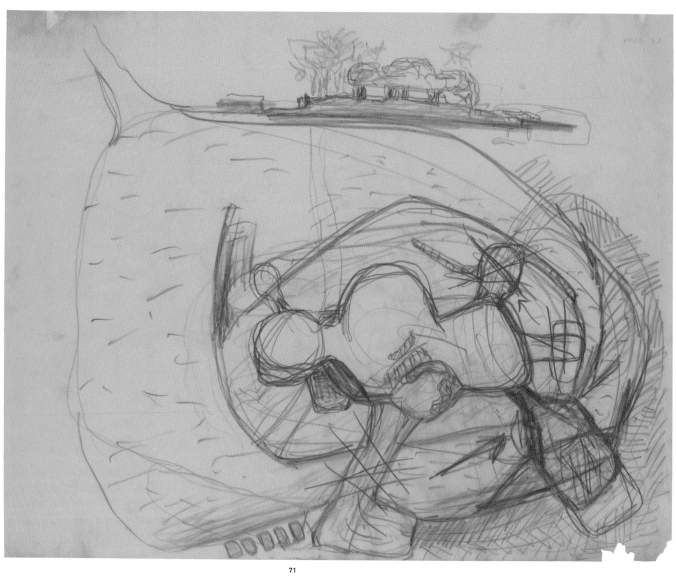

71

71–72 STUDIE ZUM *SISLER HOUSE*, 1961

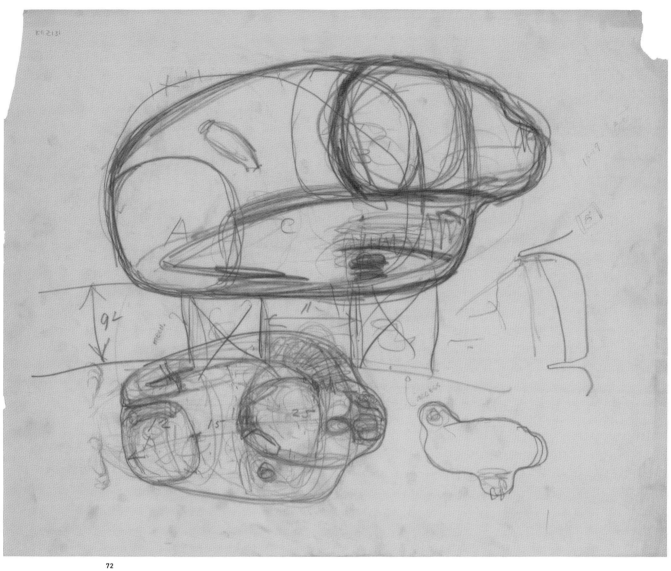

72

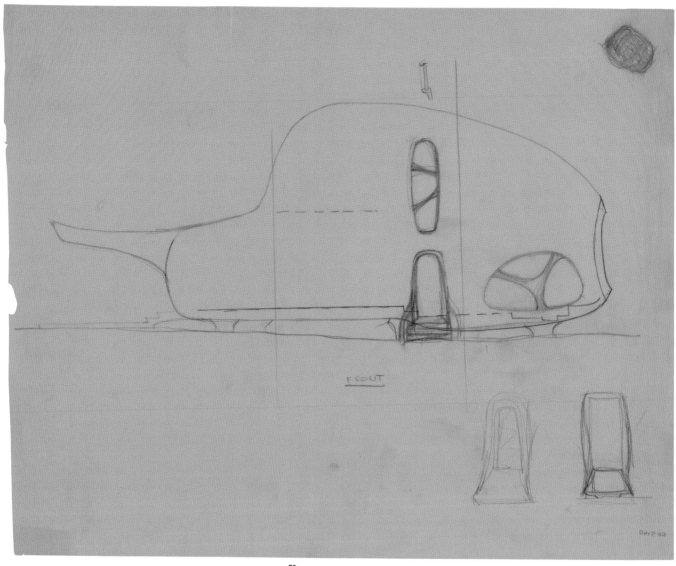

FRONT

73-74 STUDIE ZUM *SISLER HOUSE*, 1961

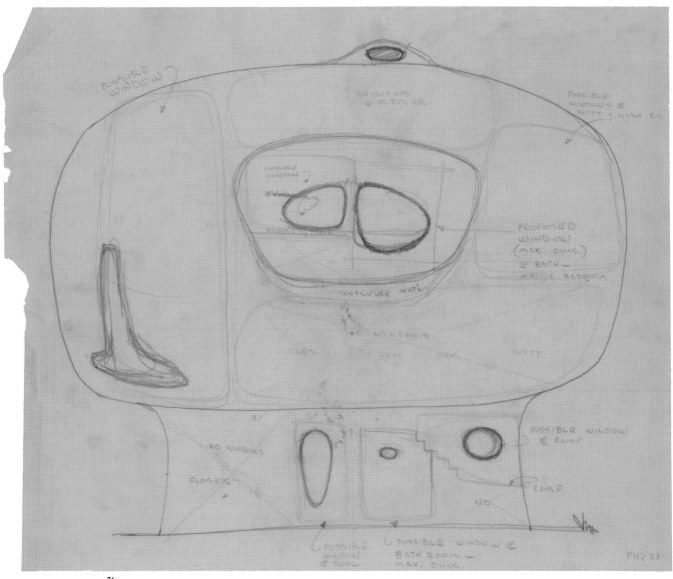

74

75 GESAMTPLAN MIT AUFRISS UND SEITENRISS, *SISLER HOUSE*, 1961

MARY SISLER HOUSE — FLORIDA U S A — FREDERICK J KIESLER ARCHITECT — 56 SEVENTH AVENUE NEW YORK CITY — DATE SEPT. 6, 1961 — SCALE ⋅ 3/16 = 3/4 — SHEET NO. 2

APPENDIX
ANHANG

VALENTINA SONZOGNI

ENDLESS HOUSE: A CHRONOLOGY [1]

ENDLESS HOUSE: EINE CHRONOLOGIE [1]

If not otherwise noted the materials are
preserved in the archive of the Frederick
Kiesler Center, Vienna.
Falls nicht anders angegeben, liegen die ausge-
wählten Materialien im Archiv des Friedrich
Kiesler-Zentrums, Wien.

1   For a detailed analysis of the
    Endless House in Kiesler's work see:
    Dieter Bogner, *Inside the Endless House*,
    Wien 1997
1   Für eine detaillierte Analyse des *Endless
    House* in Kieslers Werk siehe: Dieter Bogner,
    Inside the Endless House, Wien 1997

PP 733-742 PSEUDO-FUNCTIONALISM IN MODERN Architecture

PARTISAN REVIEW

PR

JULY, 1949

BREWSTER GHISELIN
    Hart Crane: Bridge Into the Sea

J. F. POWERS
    St. Paul, Home of the Saints

SIDNEY HOOK
    Paris Conference

PHILIP RAHV
    The Unfuture of Utopia

BRYAN MacMAHON
    Two Stories of Ireland

WYLIE SYPHER
    Nietzsche and Socrates in Messina

FREDERICK KIESLER
    Pseudo-Functionalism in Modern
    Architecture

ROBERT GORHAM DAVIS
    Culture, Religion, and Mr. Eliot

7

60c

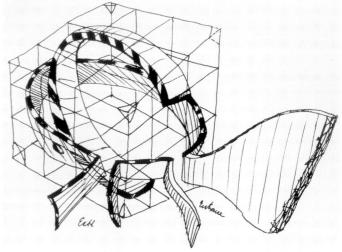

76 KIESLER AND HANS ARP, AROUND 1950
   KIESLER UND HANS ARP, UM 1950
77 *PARTISAN REVIEW*, COVER, JULY 1949
   ***PARTISAN REVIEW*, UMSCHLAG, JULI 1949**
78 SKETCH FOR *SALLE DES SUPERSTITIONS*, 1947
   SKIZZE FÜR *SALLE DES SUPERSTITIONS*, 1947

1926

At the *International Theatre Exposition* in New York, Kiesler exhibits an egg-shaped prototype and some blueprints of the floor plan for a theatre called *Endless*.

1926

Bei der *International Theatre Exposition* in New York präsentiert Kiesler einen eiförmigen Prototypen sowie Grundrissentwürfe für ein Theater, das er *Endless* nennt.

1933

Kiesler builds a full scale model of a one-family house, the *Space House*, in the Modernage Furniture Company in New York. While Kiesler uses the typical shape of the functionalist suburban house, he avoids its interior division by walls: the only way of separating the rooms are rubber curtains sliding on rails. For this project, he conceives a new building technique in-spired by natural forms such as the egg's shell.

1933

Kiesler baut ein 1:1-Modell eines Einfamilienhauses, das *Space House*, im Geschäftslokal der Modernage Furniture Company in New York. Während Kiesler die typische Gestalt des funktionalen Vorstadtheims beibehält, vermeidet er dessen innere Unterteilung durch Wände: die einzige Art der Raumtrennung sind Kunststoffvorhänge auf Gleitschienen. Für dieses Projekt ersinnt er eine neue Bautechnik, die sich durch Formen aus der Natur, etwa die Eischale, inspirieren lässt.

January/March 1934

»Notes on Architecture. The Space-House: Annotations at Random«.[2] In this text Kiesler explains his theory of *Time-Space-Architecture* and the future development of the one-family-house based on a shell-construction method.

1940s

Kiesler starts working on an unpublished book titled *Magic Architecture*, an anthology of architecture from ancient times to 20th Century including a large iconographical documentation of Kiesler's European and American visual influences.

Januar/März 1934

Es erscheint »Notes on Architecture. The Space-House: Annotations at Random«.[2] In diesen Notizen erläutert Kiesler seine Theorie der *Zeit-Raum-Architektur* und die weitere Entwicklung des Einfamilienhauses auf Basis einer Schalenbauweise.

40er-Jahre

Kiesler beginnt die Arbeit an seinem bisher unveröffentlichten Buchentwurf *Magic Architecture*, einer Anthologie der Architektur vom Altertum bis ins 20. Jahrhundert. Der Text enthält eine umfassende ikonografische Dokumentation von Kieslers europäischen und amerikanischen visuellen Einflüssen.

February 1944

A photocollage by Kiesler titled »Endless House - Space House«[3] is published in the magazine *VVV*. For the first time[4] the name *Endless House* appears in Kiesler's theory.

Winter 1946

Kiesler's »Art and Architecture: Notes on the Spiral Theme in Recent Architecture« appears in *Partisan Review*.[5]

→ see picture 77
→ siehe Abb. 77

Februar 1944

Eine Fotocollage Kieslers, betitelt »Endless House – Space House«[3], erscheint in der Zeitschrift *VVV*. Zum ersten Mal[4] taucht in Kieslers Theorie der Name *Endless House* auf.

Winter 1946

Kieslers »Art and Architecture: Notes on the Spiral Theme in Recent Architecture« erscheint in der *Partisan Review*.[5]

1947

Frederick Kiesler writes »Manifeste du Corréalisme« where his theory of *Correalism* is first introduced.[6] The article will be published two years later in *L'Architecture d'Aujourd'hui*.

May 27, 1947

Kiesler flies to Paris to design and set up the *Exposition Internationale du Surréalisme*[7] including his *Salle des superstitions*. In Paris he sketches some proposals for a *Maison en trois d'étaches*[8] [sic] in which he attempts to define a new interior space.[9]

→ see pictures 78, 80
→ siehe Abb. 78, 80

1947

Friedrich Kiesler verfasst das »Manifeste du Corréalisme«, in dem er seine Theorie des *Correalismus* vorstellt.[6] Der Text erscheint zwei Jahre später in *L'Architecture d'Aujourd'hui*.

27. Mai 1947

Kiesler fliegt nach Paris, um die *Exposition Internationale du Surréalisme*[7] einschließlich seiner *Salle des Superstitions* zu gestalten und aufzubauen. In Paris entstehen Studien zu einer *Maison en trois d'étaches*[8] [sic], wo er versucht, eine neue Form des Innenraums zu definieren.[9]

2 In: *Hound and Horn*, vol. 6, no. 3, January/March 1934, p. 292–297
2 In: *Hound and Horn*, Bd. 6, No. 3, Januar/März 1934, S. 292–297

3 In: *VVV* no. 4, 1944. The same photocollage was used for the cover of »Manifeste du Corréalisme«, published in 1949.
3 In: *VVV* No. 4, 1944. Dieselbe Fotocollage wurde für das Cover des 1949 erschienenen »Manifeste du Corréalisme« verwendet.
4 In: D. Bogner, *Friedrich Kiesler 1890–1965*, Wien 1988, p. 115
4 In: D. Bogner, *Friedrich Kiesler 1890–1965*, Wien 1988, S. 115
5 In: *Partisan Review*, winter 1946
5 In: *Partisan Review*, Winter 1946

6 In: *L'Architecture d'Aujourd'hui*, June 2, 1949, pp. 80–105
6 In: *L'Architecture d'Aujourd'hui*, 2. Juni 1949, S. 80–105
7 Dieter Bogner analyzed Kiesler's exhibition design in its relationship to the interior of the *Endless House*, which was coming together in Kiesler's mind at the time.
7 Dieter Bogner sah in Kieslers Ausstellungsdesign das Experimentierfeld für die Innenraumgestaltung des *Endless House*, das zu der Zeit in Kieslers Gedanken immer konkretere Formen annahm.
8 *Maison en trois étages*
8 *Maison en trois étages*
9 After the *Maison en trois étages* Kiesler started a series of drawings for the *Tooth House*. The drawings, dated around 1950, were inspired by natural forms, namely teeth.
9 Nach dem *Maison en trois étages* begann Kiesler eine Reihe von Zeichnungen für das *Tooth House*. Die aus der Zeit um 1950 stammenden Skizzen wurden inspiriert durch Formen der Natur, in diesem Fall durch Zähne.

July 7, 1947
Opening of the *Salle des superstitions*. Hans Arp writes an article titled »L'œuf de Kiesler et la salle des superstitions«[10] describing Kiesler's work in terms of its visual relationship to the shape of the egg.

July 1949
Frederick Kiesler publishes »Pseudo-Functionalism in Modern Architecture« where he discusses an alternative development for architectural theory and practice.[11]

→ see picture 76
→ Siehe Abb. 76

7. Juli 1947
Eröffnung der *Salle des Superstitions*. Hans Arp verfasst den Artikel »L'œuf de Kiesler et la salle des superstitions«[10], in dem er Kieslers Werk und dessen optischen Bezug zur Eiform beschreibt.

Juli 1949
Friedrich Kiesler veröffentlicht »Pseudo-Functionalism in Modern Architecture« und erörtert darin einen alternativen Entwicklungsprozess für Theorie und Praxis der Architektur.[11]

October 1, 1950
A. B. Louchheim writes in *The New York Times* an article titled: »Architect, Painter – and the Mural«. The author comments profusely the different works by Motherwell and Gottlieb as well as Hans Hofmann's decoration for a tower by José Louis Sert that was presented in the exhibition *The Muralist and the Modern Architect*. In the same article she ignores the Kiesler and Hare collaboration.[12] Another journalist, Doris Bryan, reports in *The Art Digest*: »For an egg-shaped house by the architect Frederick Kiesler, sculptor David Hare proposes a bronze staircase leading to a bronze grotto which all but fills the interior. It would be a wonderful place to visit, but I'd hate to live there.«[13]

1. Oktober 1950
A. B. Louchheim veröffentlicht in *The New York Times* den Artikel »Architect, Painter – and the Mural«. Die Autorin äußert sich darin überschwänglich zu den verschiedenen Arbeiten Motherwells und Gottliebs sowie zu dem von Hans Hofmanns dekorierten Turm José Louis Serts, der in der Ausstellung *The Muralist and The Modern Architect* gezeigt wurde, lässt jedoch die Zusammenarbeit von Kiesler und Hare unerwähnt.[12] Eine andere Journalistin, Doris Bryan, in *The Art Digest*: »Für ein eiförmiges Haus des Architekten Friedrich Kiesler schlägt der Bildhauer David Hare eine Bronzetreppe vor, die in eine bronzene Höhle führt, die fast den gesamten Innenraum ausmacht. Es wäre ein wundervoller Ort für Besuche, dort wohnen möchte ich allerdings nicht.«[13]

October 3, 1950
Opening of the exhibition *The Muralist and the Modern Architect* at the Kootz Gallery in New York. The show features some examples of modern architecture together with the works of different sculptors. The total number of architectural models displayed by Kiesler is unknown[14] but the first clay model of the *Endless House* was certainly made for this exhibition[15] and was probably shown together with a concrete shell supported by steel beams on which a David Hare sculpture was placed.[16] All those models were most probably made at the same time.[17]

3. Oktober 1950
Eröffnung der Ausstellung *The Muralist and The Modern Architect* in der Kootz Gallery in New York. Gezeigt werden Beispiele moderner Architektur neben den Arbeiten verschiedener Bildhauer. Die genaue Zahl von Kieslers ausgestellten Architekturmodellen ist unbekannt[14], mit Sicherheit wurde jedoch das erste Ton-Modell des *Endless House* für diese Schau gebaut[15] und vermutlich neben einer Schale aus Zement auf Stahlträgern ausgestellt, auf die eine Skulptur des Bildhauers David Hare gesetzt war.[16] Alle Modelle entstanden wahrscheinlich um dieselbe Zeit.[17]

October 6, 1950
A journalist reports in *Art News*: »(...) we shall probably never see this gigantic but scaleless peeble-with-picture-windows loom over some trimmed lawn.«[18]

6. Oktober 1950
Ein Journalist berichtet in *Art News*: »(...) vermutlich werden wir diesen gigantischen, aber Maßstab auflösenden Kieselstein mit Panoramafenstern nie über gepflegtem Rasen schweben sehen.«[18]

October 13, 1950
B. F. Dolbin writes in *Aufbau*: »Are Kiesler architectonical ideas feasible nowadays? One could describe them as architecture of the future, as an ideal aim to be reached in a world where not the majority, but the individual is the standard measure. We know for sure that the beneficiaries of Kiesler's ideas, will get more material reward than these uncompromising thinkers.«[19]

13. Oktober 1950
B. F. Dolbin schreibt in *Aufbau*: »Ob die Baugedanken Kieslers heute praktikabel sind? Man könnte sie als Zukunftsarchitektur bezeichnen, als ein zu erstrebendes ideales Ziel in einer Welt, deren Maß das Individuum und nicht die Masse ist. Das eine scheint uns gewiss: dass die Nutznießer der Kieslerschen Ideen mehr materiellen Erfolg ernten werden als dieser kompromissfeindliche Vordenker.«[19]

10 In: *Cahiers d'Art*, XXII, 1947, pp. 281–284
10 In: *Cahiers d'Art*, XXII, 1947, S. 281–284
11 »Pseudo-Functionalism in Modern Architecture«, in: *Partisan Review*, July 1949, pp. 733–742
11 »Pseudo-Functionalism in Modern Architecture«, in: *Partisan Review*, Juli 1949, S. 733–742

12 A. B. Louchheim, »Architect, Painter and the Mural«, in: *New York Times*, October 1, 1950
12 A. B. Louchheim, »Architect, Painter and the Mural«, in: *New York Times*, 1. Oktober 1950
13 D. Bryan, »Dealers Help Artists to Help Themselves«, in: *The Art Digest*, October 1, 1950
13 D. Bryan, »Dealers Help Artists to Help Themselves«, in: *The Art Digest*, 1. Oktober 1950

14 While most of the scholars do not discuss this particular issue, Dieter Bogner writes: »Earlier, in the *Salle des Superstitions* in Paris, Kiesler had placed one of David Hare's sculptures on top of the central element which configured the overall space. However, the combination of architecture and sculpture to which Hare aspired could only be put into practice in a limited way, since Kiesler's model was too small and the essentially larger variation designed by Hare, assembled from various segments, did not win Kiesler's approval. Two photomontages which set out to show the combination of architecture and sculpture provide some clues to the probable appereance of the version created and very probably destroyed by the sculptor.« From: D. Bogner, *Inside the Endless House*, p. 21
14 Während die meisten Wissenschaftler sich zu diesem speziellen Punkt nicht äußerten, schreibt Dieter Bogner: »Bereits in der Pariser *Salle des Superstitions* hatte Kiesler eine Arbeit

des Bildhauers [David Hare] auf die Spitze des zentralen, den Raum gestaltenden Elements gesetzt. Die von Hare angestrebte Kombination von Architektur und Skulptur konnte jedoch nur bedingt realisiert werden, da sich Kieslers Modell als viel zu klein erwies und eine von David Hare hergestellte, aus mehreren Segmenten zusammengesetzte, wesentlich größere Variante nicht die Zustimmung des Architekten fand. Einzige Rückschlüsse auf das Aussehen der mit größter Wahrscheinlichkeit zerstörten Version des Bildhauers gewähren zwei Fotos, die die Verbindung von Architektur und Skulptur veranschaulichen sollten.« In: D. Bogner, *Inside the Endless House*, S. 12
15 The Museum of Modern Art in New York purchased this model and some related drawings in 1951. The clay model is composed of a triangular-shaped base on which the lower half of the »egg« is placed. A carved and molded removable lid is placed on the lower half.

15 1951 erwarb das New Yorker Museum of Modern Art dieses Modell sowie einige dazugehörige Zeichnungen. Das Modell aus Ton besteht aus einer dreieckigen Basis, auf der die untere Hälfte des »Eis« ruht. Auf ihr sitzt ein bearbeiteter und modellierter, abnehmbarer Deckel.
16 There are two photographs in the Kiesler Archive (see page 57, left) that might be related to the first »lost« *Endless House*, showing only a portion of the shell that opens into a space partly occupied by a David Hare sculpture. A record of this »lost« *Endless House* is in: F. Kiesler, *Inside the Endless House. Art, People and Architecture. A Journal*, p. 21. See entry July 25, 1956 in this text and related note.
16 Das Kiesler-Archiv besitzt zwei Fotografien (siehe Seite 57, links), die mit diesem ersten, verlorenen Modell des *Endless House* in Zusammenhang stehen könnten; sie zeigen einen Ausschnitt der Schale, die sich zu einem

79 KIESLER AT THE NEW YORK ZOO, 1950s
KIESLER IM NEW YORKER TIERGARTEN, 50ER-JAHRE
80 KIESLER (SITTING IN THE FIRST ROW) AT THE *EXPOSITION*
INTERNATIONALE DU SURRÉALISME, PARIS 1947
KIESLER (VORNE SITZEND) BEI DER *EXPOSITION*
***INTERNATIONALE DU SURRÉALISME,* PARIS 1947**

Raum hin öffnet, der teilweise von einer Skulptur David Hares eingenommen wird. Aufzeichnungen zu diesem verschollenen Modell des *Endless House* finden sich in: F. Kiesler, *Inside the Endless House. Art, People and Architecture. A Journal,* S. 21. Siehe den Eintrag 25. Juli 1956 in diesem Text sowie die dazugehörende Fußnote.
17 In the article »Architecture Plus«, in: *Quick,* October 9, 1950, a photograph of the lost model and one of the first »egg« model are published on the same page. Kiesler reports the exhibition as follows: »In 1950 the Kootz Gallery had an exhibition of the work of sculptors, painters and architects who had made common projects. [...] David Hare, the sculptor, asked me ›Could you design a house for me so that I can make a sculpture in relation to it and we can exhibit together?‹ [...] ›I can make you a one-family version of the *Endless House,* and since one enters the *Endless* from underneath near the center, there is a chance of

making a beautifully sculpted staircase‹. I made the model, with a launching pad for it to rest on [...] David decided to enlarge the model to about five times its size [...] although it was apparently the same shape and form, it was not the same thing. Strange, we both were stunned and worried. The *Endless House,* you see, isn't it like a square house that is square anyway, no matter how long or high ... Here the calculation of the inclinations of every part must be exact, otherwise the co-ordination of the whole doesn't work. ›I don't think‹ – David admitted – ›we should exhibit this mo-del, and there is no time to do another one. Let's exhibit the little one, and at the side of it we will have the staircase in a larger scale.‹ And so it was. Small as it was, Philip Johnson acquired it for the Museum of Modern Art.« From: »Kiesler's Pursuit of an Idea« (Thomas H. Creighton interviews Frederick Kiesler), in: *Progressive Architecture,* July 1961

17 Der Artikel »Architecture Plus«, in: *Quick,* 9. Oktober 1950, bringt eine Fotografie des verloren gegangenen Modells sowie eine des ersten Tonmodells auf derselben Seite. Kiesler beschreibt das Ereignis mit folgenden Worten: »1950 präsentierte die Kootz Gallery Werke von Bildhauern, Malern und Architekten, die an gemeinsamen Projekten gearbeitet hatten [...] David Hare, der Bildhauer, fragte mich: ›Können Sie ein Haus für mich entwerfen, damit ich eine dazupassende Skulptur schaffen kann, die wir dann gemeinsam ausstellen?‹ [...] ›Ich kann eine Einfamilienversion des *Endless House* für Sie machen, und da man das *Endless* unten von der Mitte her betritt, bietet sich hier eine schöne skulpturale Treppe an.‹ Ich baute das Modell mit einer Rampe, auf der es ruht [...] David beschloss, das Modell aufs Fünffache zu vergrößern. [...] Obwohl es anscheinend dieselbe Form und Gestalt hatte, war es nicht dasselbe. Seltsam, wir waren beide

erstaunt und besorgt. Das *Endless House,* müssen Sie verstehen, ist nicht wie ein rechteckiges Haus, das rechteckig bleibt, egal, wie lang oder hoch es ist ... Hier muss die Berechnung der Neigungen überall stimmen, sonst funktioniert das Zusammenspiel des Ganzen nicht. ›Ich glaube nicht‹, gab David zu, ›dass wir dieses Modell ausstellen sollten, und wir haben keine Zeit, ein neues zu bauen. Zeigen wir das kleine, und die Treppe im größeren Maßstab stellen wir daneben.‹ Und so geschah es. Klein wie es war, erwarb Philip Johnson es für das Museum of Modern Art.« Aus: »Kiesler's Pursuit of an Idea« (Thomas H. Creightons Interview mit F. Kiesler), in: *Progressive Architecture,* Juli 1961

18 »Painters and Architects«, in: *Art News,* October 1950, no. 6
18 »Painters and Architects«, in: *Art News,* Oktober 1950, No. 619
B. F. Dolbin, »Architektur und Bildende Kunst«, in: *Aufbau,* October 13, 1950
19 B. F. Dolbin, »Architektur und Bildende Kunst«, in: *Aufbau,* 13. Oktober 1950

October 15, 1950
Kiesler holds a lecture at the Kootz Gallery on the theme *The Muralist and the Modern Architect*.[20]

November 1950
Kiesler publishes »The Endless House and Its Psychological Lighting«[21] where he stresses the importance of the lighting system in the *Endless House*.

January 1, 1951
Kiesler is awarded »Architect of the Year«[22] by the United States Television Channel CBS.

August 27–October 13, 1952
The *Endless House* is exhibited with a model of Buckminster Fuller's *Geodesic Dome* in the exhibition *Two Houses: New Ways to Build* at the Museum of Modern Art in New York.

September 14, 1952
Kiesler writes to Arthur Drexler to complain about the fact that the floor plan of the *Endless House* is not exhibited with the model: »As a matter of fact, I was unable to answer the questions from the visitors as to the interior arrangement, exact location of kitchen, dining area etc. (...) The house must, under such conditions, look to them like a haphazardous concoction. It is not.«[23]

September 15, 1952
An anonymous reporter describes the *Endless House* in the magazine *Time*: »The *Endless House*, an ellipse – shaped model somewhat resembling a large smooth stone, is the work of Vienna-born Frederick Kiesler (...) Possible cost of an *Endless House*: $ 60.000 to $ 75.000. (...) a set of prisms called a color clock, which peers out of the roof like an observatory telescope, catches the sun's rays and reflects the spectrum colors into the house; as the sun's position changes, so do the refracted colors. Conceivably, *Endless House* owners would be able to tell time by the color clock, e.g. ›half-past blue‹, ›a quarter to pink‹, ›yellow-15‹.«[24]

October 11, 1952
The *New Yorker* publishes a long article on the exhibition *Two Houses: New Ways to Build* where Buckminster Fuller is described as a technocrat in opposition to Kiesler described as an artist: »[*The Endless House*] looks like an ostrich egg perched on an irregular outcrop of rock, or a meringue with a higher upper shell separated by a horizontal division from a shallow lower shell.«[25]

15. Oktober 1950
Kiesler referiert in der Kootz Gallery zum Thema *The Muralist and the Modern Architect*.[20]

November 1950
Kiesler veröffentlicht »The Endless House and Its Psychological Lighting«[21], in dem er die Bedeutung des Beleuchtungssystems im *Endless House* betont.

1. Januar 1951
Kiesler wird vom amerikanischen Fernsehsender CBS zum »Architekten des Jahres«[22] gekürt.

27. August – 13. Oktober 1952
Das *Endless House* wird gemeinsam mit einem Modell von Buckminster Fullers *Geodätischer Kuppel* in der Ausstellung *Two Houses: New Ways to Build* im Museum of Modern Art in New York gezeigt.

14. September 1952
Kiesler beschwert sich in einem Brief an Arthur Drexler, dass der Grundriss des *Endless House* nicht gemeinsam mit dem Modell ausgestellt wird: »Tatsächlich war es mir unmöglich, auf Fragen der Besucher nach der inneren Anordnung, der genauen Position von Küche, Essbereich etc. zu antworten. (...) Das Haus muss ihnen unter solchen Umständen wie eine planlose Spielerei erscheinen. Das ist es nicht.«[23]

15. September 1952
Ein ungenannt bleibender Reporter beschreibt das *Endless House* im Magazin *Time*: »Das *Endless House*, ein ellipsenförmiges Modell, das an einen großen glatten Stein erinnert, ist das Werk des in Wien geborenen Frederick Kiesler. (...) Mögliche Kosten eines *Endless House*: 60.000 bis 75.000 $. (...) Ein Satz Prismen, genannt Farbuhr, der wie das Teleskop eines Observatoriums aus dem Dach lugt, fängt die Sonnenstrahlen ein und reflektiert die Farben des Spektrums ins Haus; mit dem Stand der Sonne verändern sich die gebrochenen Farben. Es ist vorstellbar, dass *Endless-House*-Besitzer die Zeit von der Farbuhr ablesen könnten, z. B. ›halb Blau‹, ›Viertel vor Pink‹, ›15 Minuten nach Gelb‹.«[24]

11. Oktober 1952
Der *New Yorker* bringt einen langen Artikel über die Ausstellung *Two Houses: New Ways to Build*, in dem Buckminster Fuller als Technokrat, Kiesler im Gegensatz dazu als Künstler beschrieben wird: »[Das *Endless House*] sieht aus wie ein Straußenei, das auf einer Felsnase hockt, oder wie ein Baiser mit einer höheren oberen Schale, die durch eine horizontale Fuge von einer flacheren unteren Schale getrennt wird.«[25]

20 D. Bogner, *Friedrich Kiesler 1890–1965*, p. 141
20 In: D. Bogner, *Friedrich Kiesler 1890–1965*, S. 141
21 »The Endless House and Its Psychological Lighting«, in: *Interiors*, November 1950, pp. 122–129. In this article Kiesler deals with artificial and natural light and the way in which it can enlarge or reduce interior space and its perception.
21 »The Endless House and Its Psychological Lighting«, in: *Interiors*, November 1950, S. 122–129. In diesem Artikel setzt Kiesler sich mit natürlichem und künstlichem Licht auseinander und mit der Art und Weise, wie es den Innenraum bzw. dessen Wahrnehmung größer oder kleiner erscheinen lassen kann.

22 See note 20
22 Siehe Fußnote 20
23 Kiesler remarks also that »Fuller's model is illustrated by an endless variety of details«. Letter to Arthur Drexler, typescript
23 Kiesler bemerkt weiter, dass »Fullers Modell durch unzählige Details veranschaulicht wird«. Brief Friedrich Kieslers an Arthur Drexler, Typoskript

24 »Beyond the Horizon«, in: *Time*, September 15, 1952, p. 68
24 »Beyond the Horizon«, in: *Time*, 15. September 1952, S. 68
25 In: *The New Yorker*, October 11, 1952, pp. 73–74. »This is [Fuller's *Geodesic Dome*] a technocrat's dream, which is another way of saying that it is a humanist's nightmare.« Kiesler: »He is less interested in pure technics than in biotechnics; that is, in the norms and conditions of life. Being an artist, he knows that the form of the structure is as significant as its function.« In spite of all that, Kiesler »tends to think of human needs in limited terms and to place the architect's yearning for original design above traditional human requirements«. In a letter to Arthur Drexler, Kiesler discusses the idea of juxtaposing the two models: »While I appreciate your idea of juxtaposing my model with that of Fuller's, his being conceived from a mechanistic point of view while mine from an esthetic one, I cannot agree with you regarding my own house. I can only state the fact that it has primarily being conceived for the creation of satisfactory living conditions, the spatial areas needed for this purpose, and that from these conditions I have

arrived at the dimensions, the form and the construction scheme. The esthetic aspect comes with it and was not the primary thought.« Letter to Arthur Drexler, typescript, see footnote 23
25 In: *The New Yorker*, 11. Oktober 1952, S. 73–74. »Es [Fullers *Geodätische Kuppel*] ist der Traum eines Technokraten, mit anderen Worten der Alptraum eines Humanisten.« Kiesler dazu: »Er interessiert sich weniger für reine Technik als für Biotechnik, d. h. die Normen und Bedingungen des Lebens. Als Künstler weiß er, dass die Form des Gebäudes ebenso wichtig ist wie seine Funktion.« Trotzdem neige Kiesler dazu, »menschliche Bedürfnisse nur beschränkt wahrzunehmen und den Wunsch des Architekten nach originellen Entwürfen über traditionelle Ansprüche des Menschen zu stellen«. In einem Brief an Arthur Drexler hinterfragt Kiesler die Sinnhaftigkeit, die beiden Modelle nebeneinander zu präsentieren: »Während ich Ihre Idee schätze, mein Modell neben dem Fullers zu zeigen, seines von einem mechanistischen Gesichtspunkt aus, meines hingegen von einem ästhetischen, kann ich Ihnen, mein eigenes Haus betreffend, nicht zustimmen. Ich kann nur betonen, dass

es in erster Linie ersonnen wurde, um befriedigende Wohnverhältnisse, die dafür nötigen Raumbereiche zu schaffen, und dass ich ausgehend davon zu den Dimensionen, der Form und der Bauweise gelangt bin. Der ästhetische Aspekt ist eine Begleiterscheinung und war nicht der vorrangige Gedanke.« Friedrich Kiesler an Arthur Drexler, Typoskript, siehe Fußnote 23
26 »As I remember, that first unit was the original model for the *Endless House*, a piece of architecture done in clay and constituting a triple interplay of shells, one hollow laid within another, like broken eggshells. Altogether they were about one and a half feet long and one foot wide. Not a sculpture, mind you, but a piece of architecture (...) the clay shells shells cracked when put into a wooden cradle for drying. (...) I decided not to let the labor of several weeks be totally lost but to take a chance and cast it in bronze, just to preserve a record of a part of the *Endless House* model.« In: Frederick Kiesler, *Inside the Endless House*, p. 21

July 25, 1956
Kiesler discusses the making of his sculpture *Vessel of Fire*, in which he claims to have placed a part of a model for the *Endless House*[26], with his first wife Steffi.

January 1957
Opening of Kiesler's and Bartos' *World House Galleries*.

February 1958
Kiesler receives a grant of $ 12.000 by the R. H. Gottesmann Foundation[27] in order to produce the model and the preliminary plans for an *Endless House* which was to be built in the garden of the Museum of Modern Art.

March 1958
Art News announces that Kiesler has received a grant to erect his *Endless House* in the garden of the Museum of Modern Art: »(...) the 40 by 60 by 25 foot structure now planned is as modern as the space satellites to which inevitably it will be compared in the press«.[28]

July 3, 1958
Kiesler writes in a letter to Piero Dorazio: »I have work to do, particularly to start modelling studies for the *Endless House* to be built by the Museum of Modern Art next spring. I haven't done anything about it and I'm under contract.«[29]

July 11, 1958
Kiesler writes a poem on the *Endless House* titled *Life is short, Art is long, Architecture endless*.[30]

September 14, 1958
He makes preliminary drawings for an *Endless House* for Chicago.[31]

April 10, 1959
Kiesler writes an eulogy for Frank Lloyd Wright where, in the space of two columns, he analyzes Wright's personality and architecture stating that: »The man who hated abstract art produced the most abstract building of our time.«[32]

25. Juli 1956
Kiesler bespricht die Entstehung seiner Skulptur *Vessel of Fire*, in der er nach eigenen Angaben einen Teil eines Modells des *Endless House* verarbeitet hat[26], mit seiner ersten Frau Steffi.

Januar 1957
Eröffnung von Kieslers und Bartos' *World House Galleries*.

Februar 1958
Kiesler erhält ein Stipendium der R. H. Gottesmann Foundation in Höhe von 12.000 $[27] für ein Modell und Vorentwürfe eines *Endless House*, das im Garten des Museum of Modern Art errichtet werden soll.

März 1958
Art News berichtet, Kiesler habe ein Stipendium erhalten, um sein *Endless House* im Garten des Museum of Modern Art zu realisieren: »(...) Das geplante, 12 m x 18 m x 7,5 m große Objekt ist modern wie die Weltraumsatelliten, mit denen es in der Presse zwangsläufig verglichen werden wird.«[28]

3. Juli 1958
In einem Brief an Piero Dorazio schreibt Kiesler: »Ich habe viel zu tun, vor allem müsste ich mit den Modellstudien für das *Endless House* beginnen, das nächsten Frühling vom Museum of Modern Art gebaut werden soll. Ich habe noch nichts gemacht und ich stehe unter Vertrag.«[29]

11. Juli 1958
Kiesler schreibt ein Gedicht über das *Endless House*: *Life is short, Art is long, Architecture endless* [Das Leben ist kurz, die Kunst ist lang, die Architektur ohne Ende].[30]

14. September 1958
Er zeichnet Vorentwürfe eines *Endless House* für Chicago.[31]

10. April 1959
Kiesler verfasst eine Eloge auf Frank Lloyd Wright; in zwei Spalten analysiert er die Persönlichkeit und Architektur Wrights und stellt fest, dass »der Mann, der die abstrakte Kunst hasste, das abstrakteste Gebäude unserer Zeit geschaffen hat«.[32]

26 »Wie ich mich erinnere, war das erste Exemplar das Originalmodell des *Endless House*, ein Stück Architektur in Ton, ein dreifaches Zusammenspiel von Schalen, ineinander liegend wie zerbrochene Eierschalen. Zusammen waren sie rund 50 Zentimeter lang und 30 Zentimeter breit. Keine Skulptur, wohlgemerkt, sondern ein Stück Architektur. (...) die Tonschalen sprangen, als sie zum Trocknen aufgelegt wurden. (...) Ich beschloss, die Arbeit mehrerer Wochen nicht ganz aufzugeben, sondern einen Versuch zu wagen und sie in Bronze zu gießen, um einen Teil des *Endless-House*-Modells zu dokumentieren und zu bewahren.« In: F. Kiesler, *Inside the Endless House*, S. 21

27 From the grant he receives in 1958 Kiesler realizes four models for an *Endless House*. The largest one is now in the Whitney Museum of American Art in New York. Another model which was also realized in 1959 is part of the Dieter and Gertraud Bogner Collection (now on permanent display at the Museum of Applied Arts in Vienna). Two shell constructions were realized in 1958/59 probably to test the limits of a wire mesh and concrete structure and were shown in *Shell Sculptures and Galaxies* at Leo Castelli's gallery in 1961. The models are now in the Jason McCoy Collection, New York.

27 Mit dem Stipendium, das er 1958 erhält, baut Kiesler vier Modelle des *Endless House*. Das größte steht nun im Whitney Museum of American Art in New York. Ein weiteres Modell, ebenfalls aus dem Jahr 1959, ist Teil der Sammlung Dieter und Gertraud Bogner (zu sehen als permanente Ausstellung im Museum für angewandte Kunst in Wien). Zwei Schalenkonstruktionen entstanden 1958/59, vermutlich, um die Grenzen einer Draht- und Betonstruktur zu testen, und wurden 1961 in der Schau *Shell Sculptures and Galaxies* in der Leo Castelli Gallery ausgestellt. Beide Modelle befinden sich nun in der Sammlung Jason McCoy, New York.
28 »Arp, de Kooning, Kiesler, Miró for Modern«, in: *Art News*, March 1958
28 »Arp, de Kooning, Kiesler, Miró for Modern«, in: *Art News*, März 1958
29 Letter to Piero Dorazio, typescript
29 Brief an Piero Dorazio, Typoskript

30 Frederick Kiesler, *Life is short, Art is long, Architecture endless*, typescript
30 Frederick Kiesler, *Life is short, Art is long, Architecture endless*, Typoskript
31 Handwritten note on a pencil drawing.
31 Handschriftliche Notiz auf einer Bleistiftzeichnung.

32 Frederick Kiesler, »Frank Lloyd Wright«, in: *It Is*, no. 4, 1959, p. 27
32 Friedrich Kiesler, »Frank Lloyd Wright«, in: *It Is*, No. 4, 1959, S. 27

May 25, 1959
In the article »Tough Prophet«, published in *Time*, the *Endless House* is described as follows: »Anchored to its supporting columns as lightly as a dirigible (...) looks more like a cloud than a building (...) Might it be also comfortable? Where would the refrigerator go? Won't those balconies be dangerous for children? How about privacy, heating and storage? Kiesler does have answers to these questions, though as an all-out idea man he can be impatient with too much insistence on the practical.«[33]

August 17, 1959
Kiesler writes to Bruno Zevi[34]: »I would like to renew my suggestion that you might perhaps talk the matter over with Mr. Olivetti, or anybody whom you might see fit to do it, or perhaps for the Triennale in Milan , but of course, I would just love to see it in Rome – simply as a natural transformation of an old Mediterranean building method into a new one. Hands across the centuries. (...) It is amazing how this project has set the architectural world on fire. I am quite sure that I will see it built somewhere by someone else before I've had a real chance at it!«

October 1959
The *Endless House* is presented in *Harper's Bazaar* in a large photograph showing Kiesler in the foreground. The article says: »Eschewing straight lines for an organic interplay of curves that appears deceptively unfamiliar (the body is, he says, the primary house), his structure is the first in history to eliminate any compression element (...) *Endless House* (...) is the triumph of individuality. It cannot be industry-built. It must be handmade.«[35]

January 1, 1960
In an article written by Arthur Drexler for *Vogue*[36], Kiesler is portrayed with his *Endless House* in an Irving Penn photograph that greatly contributed to Kiesler's fame.

February 1960
Art News presents new trends in architecture for the year to come. One of the new paths in architecture is the organic free form: »Some look like great birds nestling to the ground, others like ancient barks in full sail, each illustrating new possibilities of enclosed space bound to no corner or square: a culmination so far is Frederick Kiesler's *Endless House*, building curled-up room enclosures together into a huge honeycomb.«[37]

---

25. Mai 1959
Im Artikel »Tough Prophet« in *Time* wird das *Endless House* folgendermaßen beschrieben: »An seinen tragenden Säulen lose verankert wie ein Luftschiff (...), gleicht es mehr einer Wolke als einem Gebäude. (...) Könnte es auch gemütlich sein? Wo käme der Kühlschrank hin? Sind diese Balkone nicht gefährlich für Kinder? Was ist mit Privatsphäre, Heizung und Stauraum? Kiesler hat auf all diese Fragen eine Antwort, obwohl er als totaler Kopfmensch über zu großem Nachdruck auf das Praktische die Geduld verlieren kann.«[33]

17. August 1959
Kiesler schreibt an Bruno Zevi[34]: »Darf ich Ihnen erneut vorschlagen, die Angelegenheit vielleicht mit Mr. Olivetti zu besprechen, oder wer immer Ihnen als geeigneter Ansprechpartner erscheint, vielleicht auch für die Triennale in Mailand, aber natürlich würde ich es liebend gerne in Rom sehen – einfach als natürliche Wandlung einer alten mediterranen Bauweise in eine neue. Hände, die sich über Jahrhunderte hinweg ausstrecken. (...) Es ist erstaunlich, wie dieses Projekt die Architekturwelt entflammt. Ich bin mir ziemlich sicher, dass ich es irgendwo von irgendwem gebaut sehe, noch bevor ich Gelegenheit dazu hatte!«

Oktober 1959
Das *Endless House* wird mit einem großformatigen Foto mit Kiesler im Vordergrund in *Harper's Bazaar* vorgestellt. Der Artikel konstatiert: »Ohne gerade Linien, stattdessen mit einem organischen Zusammenspiel von Kurven, das trügerisch unvertraut erscheint (der Körper, sagt er, ist das ursprüngliche Haus), ist sein Gebäude das erste in der Geschichte, das auf jedes in eine Form gepresste Element verzichtet. (...) Das *Endless House* (...) ist der Triumph der Individualität. Man kann es nicht industriell erzeugen. Es muss von Hand gefertigt werden.«[35]

1. Januar 1960
In einem Artikel Arthur Drexlers für *Vogue*[36] erscheint Kiesler mit seinem *Endless House* auf einem Foto von Irving Penn, das Kiesler bekannt machte.

Februar 1960
Art News stellt Architekturtrends für das kommende Jahr vor. Eine der neuen Richtungen in der Architektur sind freie organische Formen: »Manche sehen aus wie große am Boden nistende Vögel, andere wie alte Barken mit vollen Segeln; alle veranschaulichen sie neue Möglichkeiten für umschlossenen Raum, der nicht zwangsweise Ecken oder Quadrate aufweisen muss: Einen Höhepunkt bis dato stellt Friedrich Kieslers *Endless House* dar, das zusammengerollte Raumbereiche zu einer riesigen Honigwabe verbaut.«[37]

---

33 »Tough Prophet«, in: *Time*, May 25, 1959
33 »Tough Prophet«, in: *Time*, 25. Mai 1959
34 The architect and critic Bruno Zevi (1918–2000) is one of the leading figure of post-war italian architecture and the founder of the architectural magazine *L'Architettura. Cronache e storia*. In 1957 he wrote an article on Kiesler's *World House Galleries* to which Kiesler reacted with a rather aggressive letter. After a difficult start, Kiesler and Zevi started a correspondence and they eventually met in Rome in the early 1960s. The plan to build the *Endless House* either for the Venice Biennale or in Rome was not realized even though encouraged and supported by Italian artists and critics like Bruno Zevi, Piero Dorazio, Giuseppe Santomaso.

34 Der Architekt und Kritiker Bruno Zevi (1918–2000) ist eine der führenden Gestalten der italienischen Nachkriegsarchitektur und Gründer der Architekturzeitschrift *L'Architettura. Cronache e storia*. 1957 verfasste er einen Artikel über Kieslers *World House Galleries*, auf den Kiesler mit einem recht aggressiven Brief reagierte. Nach diesem schwierigen Auftakt begannen Kiesler und Zevi zu korrespondieren und lernten sich schließlich Anfang der sechziger Jahre in Rom kennen. Der Plan, das *Endless House* entweder für die Biennale in Venedig oder in Rom zu bauen, wurde trotz Ermutigung und Unterstützung von italienischen Künstlern und Kritikern wie Bruno Zevi, Piero Dorazio und Giuseppe Santomaso nicht umgesetzt.

35 »New Concepts of Architecture«, in: *Harper's Bazaar*, October 1959
35 »New Concepts of Architecture«, in: *Harper's Bazaar*, Oktober 1959

36 Arthur Drexler, »Frederick Kiesler and His Endless House«, in: *Vogue*, January 1, 1960
36 Arthur Drexler, »Frederick Kiesler and His Endless House«, in: *Vogue*, 1. Januar 1960

37 »Editorial. A cityscape for the 1960s«, in: *Art News*, February 1960
37 »Editorial. A cityscape for the 1960s«, in: *Art News*, Februar 1960

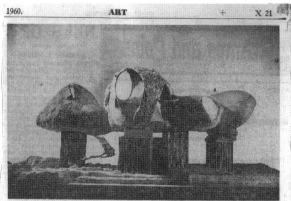

1960.   ART   +   X 21

GLIMPSE OF FUTURE?—Model of Frederick Kiesler's Endless House, in the Museum of Modern Art's exhibition, "Visionary Architecture," which opened last week. Until Dec. 4.

THE ARCHITECT AS A PROPHET

By ADA LOUISE HUXTABLE

A FAR-OUT show has just opened at the Museum of Modern Art that promises to be the season's shocker. For an institution that has led us to expect the spectacular, in a city as inured to sensation as New York, this isn't an easy accomplishment. But "Visionary Architecture," the exhibition that will be on view in the Museum's third floor galleries through Dec. 4, contains all of the necessary elements. It has a dizzying idea, architectural schemes of stupefying scope and murky psychological undertones, and, as usual, a dramatic installation.

Architects' Dreams

The theme of the show is staggering. "Visionary Architecture" is a round-up of this century's most extreme and esoteric proposals for remaking the world. (Architects have never been noted for false modesty.) It ranges from huge projects for whole cities that would make Buck Rogers blush, to a vast undertaking for remodeling the Alps—a kind of architectural improvement on God. This is the designer's dream-life, the landscape of the imagination, the unbuilt imagery of the conscious and subconscious mind.

If the visitor comes away reeling, he has plenty to think about. For like many of the Museum's shockers, the show also has impressive content. These schemes—none of which, needless to say, exists—are provocative in the most grand and giddy sense. First, they suggest unexplored technological and esthetic horizons. Second, they offer the broadest possible investigation of socio-architectural problems unhampered by society's present standards and solutions, which, in the case of our strangling cities and devastated countryside, are usually no solutions at all. And third, they present patterns of the future beyond any conventional contemporary concept.

Prominent Theorists

Some of the most respected architectural theorists and philosophers of the twentieth century are present—Le Corbusier, Frank Lloyd Wright, Lou Kahn, Frederick Kiesler, Buckminster Fuller. Moreover, the import of their dreams is inescapable. These men, all of whom are well-versed in practical construction, are here more concerned with the question of what we should build, than with how we should built it. In an age when technology has become an aim in itself and an excuse for everything, including style, they use it only as a means to an end. They fly dangerously high, but they dare to probe the deeper meanings of architectural expression.

At best, however, the answers are never more than abstract exercises. Their frequent pretentiousness and patent impracticability will annoy as much as titillate—an unbeatable combination at the box office. Proposals range from quasi-to absolute, to outrageous improbability. For Algiers, Le Corbusier has designed a nine-mile long, fourteen-story high building that doubles as a super-

highway. With the help of life-size photographs, the spectator can enter Frederick Kiesler's world of "endless space," a kind of free-form Fun House, or gelatinous Cabinet of Dr. Caligari. A dramatic series of enlargements present Bruno Taut's 1919 fantasy of classic megalomaniac grandeur—a vista of Alpine peaks cut, polished, faceted and trimmed to suit his own esthetic vision of the Universe.

The dreams of the young, as usual, are particularly dazzling. A "Bio-Technical City," designed by Paolo Soleri for the Arizona Mesa, proposes a series of monumental, plant-like structures connected by underground caverns for churches, museums, or "just beautiful spaces." Not the least of its extraordinary features is the architect's original drawing (not shown), an incredible 200-feet long. A young Japanese, Kiyonori Kikutake, has come up with one of the most intriguing concepts of all—a "Marine City" consisting of floating concrete cylinders containing dwellings with underwater views (the symbolism becomes increasingly terrifying) based on the not untenable theory that future population expansion may force communities into the sea. Significantly, a good number of these projects are concerned with the city—the most pressing problem of our time.

The organization of the exhibition is as remarkable as the material. The architectural images are grouped in two startling, non-architectural categories: Mountains and Roads. "There is a recurrent pattern

in this kind of work, a basic consistency," explains Arthur Drexler, Director of the Museum's Department of Architecture, who has conceived, directed and installed the show. "Architectural visions almost invariably follow one of two types," he observes, "mountain-concepts, which are towering, pyramidal schemes, or road-concepts, where road and buildings become one, as a continuous design between two points."

Idea and Realization

Mr. Drexler, who assumed his directorship at the early age of 31 in 1956, has been responsible for many of the challenging shows that have helped insure the Museum's avant-garde reputation. He feels that "Visionary Architecture," in spite of its "mad scientist" connotations and its accent on sensationalism, is a serious, attention-worthy subject. "The importance of this exhibition is that we show the architectural idea—the image—as it comes from the designer in its purest state. Today, the architect's concept far outreaches what the community will accept. Here there is no gap between the idea and its realization. For the architect, this is the child's idea of bliss—a mountain of ice cream."

The flavors will hardly be to everyone's taste. The effect of this strange, sometimes sinister show, containing equal parts of genius, arrogance and just plain foolishness, is as disturbing as it is stimulating. But if it provides a small, sharp jolt toward more profound architectural thinking, the museum can chalk up another success.

81

83

81 FREDERICK KIESLER IN FRONT OF A TEMPLE, AROUND 1958
    FRIEDRICH KIESLER VOR EINEM TEMPEL, UM 1958
82 »THE ARCHITECT AS A PROPHET«, IN: *TIME*, MAY 25, 1959
    »THE ARCHITECT AS A PROPHET«, IN: *TIME*, 25. MAI 1959
83 KIESLER WITH LEO CASTELLI (MIDDLE) AND
    SALVATORE SCARPITTA (RIGHT), AROUND 1960
    **KIESLER MIT LEO CASTELLI (MITTE) UND
    SALVATORE SCARPITTA (RECHTS), UM 1960**

April 1960
Exhibition of drawings for the *Endless House* at the Great Jones Gallery.

February 8, 1960
Kiesler writes a telegram to Bruno Zevi: »Happy to tell you that money now available to erect *Endless House* in Venice or Rome this summer, to be moved later to U.S. Wonder if you could help solve location problem.«[38]

March 20, 1960
Kiesler is interviewed for the television show »Camera Three« where he talks about the theory, the project and the models of the *Endless House*.

March 27, 1960
Ada Louise Huxtable reports her impressions on Kiesler's interview on television: »Mr. Kiesler has a singular talent. He is a master of intellectual persuasion, an esthetic salesman on an almost evangelical level. (...) We are sure that the post and beam has had its day, that the right angle is dead, that square shelters are square and the people in them, squarer. (...) To this observer, entering a Kiesler creation provides the momentary pleasure of being inside an up-dated, abstract easter egg, followed by the frustration of unnecessary and unjustifiable disturbances and distractions, and a longing for the simplicity and logic of plane surfaces and straight lines. The basic fallacy is that Mr. Kiesler's concept of architecture is not really architecture (...) But unfortunately, Mr. Kiesler has another talent – not quite so rare. He continually disproves what he says by what he does. Put into practice, his theories tend to be refuted by their execution.«[39]

April 17, 1960
Kiesler writes to the editor of the *Sunday Times*: »In an article on Sunday March 27, you quote Mr. Philip Johnson's double-edged compliment naming me as the ›greatest non-building architect of our time‹ (...) I still feel that it is better to concentrate on a few honest possibilities to build and otherwise wait, unconcerned at being named ›the greatest non-building architect of our time‹, than to be, as it sometimes the case, ›a most-building non-architect‹.«[40]

April 20, 1960
Kiesler meets with a member of the advisory board of the Museum of Modern Art to discuss the reasons why the construction of the *Endless House* is continuously being postponed.[41]

---

8. Februar 1960
Kiesler in einem Telegramm an Bruno Zevi: »Freue mich mitzuteilen, dass Geld vorhanden für Bau des *Endless House* diesen Sommer in Venedig oder Rom und spätere Überstellung in die Staaten. Bräuchte Ihre Hilfe bei Standortsuche.«[38]

20. März 1960
Kiesler wird für die Fernsehshow »Camera Three« interviewt und erklärt Theorie, Projekt und Modelle des *Endless House*.

27. März 1960
Ada Louise Huxtable schildert ihre Eindrücke nach Kieslers Fernsehinterview: »Mr. Kiesler besitzt ein einzigartiges Talent. Er ist ein Meister der intellektuellen Überzeugungsarbeit, ein Verkäufer von Ästhetik mit fast schon missionarischem Sendungsbewusstsein. (...) Wir sind sicher, dass Pfeiler und Balken der Vergangenheit angehören, dass der rechte Winkel tot ist, dass viereckige Behausungen spießig sind und die Leute, die darin wohnen, noch spießiger. (...) Dieser Beobachterin bot der Besuch einer Kreation Kieslers das momentane Vergnügen, ein hypermodernes, abstraktes Osterei zu betreten, gefolgt von der Frustration über unnötige und ungerechtfertigte Störungen und Ablenkungen und der Sehnsucht nach der Schlichtheit und Logik von ebenen Oberflächen und geraden Linien. Der grundlegende Irrtum liegt darin, dass Mr. Kieslers Architekturbegriff nicht wirklich Architektur ist. (...) Unglücklicherweise hat Mr. Kiesler ein weiteres Talent – ein gar nicht so seltenes. Er widerlegt das, was er sagt, ständig durch das, was er tut. In die Praxis umgesetzt, werden seine Theorien häufig von ihrer Ausführung entkräftet.«[39]

April 1960
Kiesler stellt seine Zeichnungen für das *Endless House* in der Great Jones Gallery aus.

17. April 1960
Kiesler schreibt an den Herausgeber der *Sunday Times*: »In einem Artikel von Sonntag, dem 27. März, zitieren sie Mr. Philip Johnsons zweischneidiges Kompliment, in dem er mich als den ›größten nicht bauenden Architekten unserer Zeit‹ bezeichnet. (...) Ich bin noch immer der Ansicht, dass es besser ist, sich auf ein paar ehrliche Möglichkeiten des Bauens zu konzentrieren und ansonsten zu warten, gleichgültig, ob man ›der größte nicht bauende Architekt unserer Zeit‹ genannt wird, als, wie es manchmal der Fall ist, ›ein meistbauender Nichtarchitekt‹ zu sein.«[40]

20. April 1960
Kiesler trifft sich mit einem Mitglied des Beratungskomitees des Museum of Modern Art, um die Gründe für die ständige Verschiebung des *Endless-House*-Baus zu erörtern.[41]

38 Telegramm from Frederick Kiesler to Bruno Zevi.
38 Telegramm Friedrich Kieslers an Bruno Zevi.

39 A. L. Huxtable, »Architecture on TV: Greatest Non-Building Architect of Our Time Expounds His Ideas«, in: *New York Times*, March 27, 1960
39 A. L. Huxtable, »Architecture on TV: Greatest Non-Building Architect of Our Time Expounds His Ideas«, in: *New York Times*, 27. März 1960

40 »To the Art Editor/Building Architect«, in: *Sunday Times*, April 17, 1960
40 »To the Art Editor/Building Architect«, in: *Sunday Times*, 17. April 1960

41 Frederick Kiesler, *Inside the Endless House*, p. 268
41 Frederick Kiesler, *Inside the Endless House*, S. 268
42 Ibid., p. 267–268
42 Ebd., S. 267–268

April 22, 1960
Kiesler reports in *Inside the Endless House*: »The chief of the tribe of the *World House Galleries* wanted the *Endless House* to be built for him on his ground in Connecticut and ready on September 27th. At the same time, he would have an exhibition of my work at his gallery thus promoting the *Endless House*.«[42] The project is not realized since the purchaser suddenly changes his mind as reported by Kiesler: »[He said:] ›I am not in a hurry. I still have my house and my children aren't going away to college until two years from now, so I won't be in the actual need of the *Endless* for two years.‹ I was shocked. I had planned the house for him on the assumption that he wanted by September 27th of this year, a five-month race to finish (...).«[43]

May 9, 1960
Kiesler reports in *Inside the Endless House*: »The plans for the Museum of Modern Art just arrived. Arthur Drexler indicated the area reserved for me and expects me to make a layout for the proposed exhibition.«[44] It is clear now that the *Endless House* won't be built as life size prototype, but will instead be presented as a smaller model.

May 26, 1960
Kiesler meets with the artist Salvatore Scarpitta and they discuss the display of the *Endless House* in an exhibition: »Scarpita [sic] gave me a blistering lecture on why I should not agree to make a midget model of the *Endless* for the exhibition at the Museum of Modern Art, particularly with all the lighting effects. I would lower the purely architectural standard of my project to the level of a theatrical display, he said, and could only gratify vulgar public taste. (...) He suggested that I use the large space to build a super-*galaxy*, a sculptural idea, an abstraction of the *Endless House*. (...) Give them a section, a cut-out piece of the total concept, but in full scale, rather than the total concept in miniature. Your work must always be hard and uncompromised.«[45]

→ see picture 83
→ Siehe Abb. 83

September 20 – December 4, 1960
The *Endless House* model[46] is shown in the exhibition *Visionary Architecture* at the Museum of Modern Art.

September 28, 1960
Kiesler writes: »Today, the day after the opening at the Museum of Modern Art which is to open the possibilities for my ›impossible‹ building, up the *Endless*, to be built – somewhere, somehow – floating on water or elevated into the air. It seemed to have been a good start, just having the model exposed. (...) My model was cruising like a flying saucer of reinforced concrete full of holes and gaps to look through, people sticking their heads in and getting nothing out of it (...).«[47] After the show Kiesler goes to P.J.Clarke's bar with some friends including the Reiss', Peggy Jackson, Luba Harrington, Sidney Janis, Leo Castelli: »Bob Rauschenberg and Jasper Johns, who were struck by the precision of my curvilinear concepts in ink of the original (1924) Vienna plans for the *Endless*«.[48]

22. April 1960
Kiesler berichtet in *Inside the Endless House*: »Der Häuptling der *World House Galleries* wollte, dass das *Endless House* auf seinem Anwesen in Connecticut gebaut wird, und zwar bis 27. September. Zur gleichen Zeit würde er dann meine Arbeit in seiner Galerie ausstellen und das *Endless House* so bewerben.«[42] Das Projekt wird nicht verwirklicht, weil der Käufer plötzlich seine Meinung ändert: »[Er sagte:] ›Ich habe keine Eile. Ich habe noch mein Haus, und meine Kinder gehen erst in zwei Jahren aufs College, daher brauche ich das *Endless* in den nächsten zwei Jahren nicht.‹ Ich war schockiert. Ich hatte das Haus für ihn in der Annahme geplant, er wolle es bis 27. September dieses Jahres fertig haben, fünf Monate Arbeit gegen die Uhr (...).«[43]

9. Mai 1960
Kiesler schreibt in *Inside the Endless House*: »Die Pläne für das Museum of Modern Art sind eben gekommen. Arthur Drexler hat den für mich reservierten Standort markiert und erwartet von mir ein Konzept für die geplante Ausstellung.«[44] Es ist jetzt klar, dass das *Endless House* nicht als Prototyp in Originalgröße gebaut, sondern als kleineres Modell gezeigt werden wird.

26. Mai 1960
Kiesler trifft den Künstler Salvatore Scarpitta und spricht mit ihm über die Präsentation des *Endless House* in einer Ausstellung: »Scarpita [sic] hielt mir einen glühenden Vortrag, warum ich nicht zustimmen sollte, ein winziges Modell des *Endless* für die Ausstellung des Museum of Modern Art zu machen, insbesondere wegen all der Beleuchtungseffekte. Ich würde den pur architektonischen Standard meines Projekts auf das Niveau einer Theaterkulisse herabwürdigen, sagte er, und könnte damit nur den ordinären öffentlichen Geschmack befriedigen. (...) Er schlug vor, dass ich den großen Raum dazu nutze, eine Super-*Galaxy*, eine plastische Idee, eine Abstraktion des *Endless House* zu bauen. (...) Geben Sie ihnen lieber einen Teil, einen Ausschnitt des ganzen Konzepts, aber das dafür in voller Größe, als das ganze Konzept in Miniatur. Ihre Arbeit muss stets hart und kompromisslos sein.«[45]

20. September – 4. Dezember 1960
Das *Endless-House*-Modell[46] wird im Rahmen der Ausstellung *Visionary Architecture* im Museum of Modern Art gezeigt.

28. September 1960
Kiesler schreibt: »Heute, am Tag nach der Ausstellungseröffnung im Museum of Modern Art, die meinem ›unmöglichen‹ Gebäude, dem *Endless*, Möglichkeiten eröffnen soll, gebaut zu werden – irgendwo, irgendwie – auf dem Wasser schwimmend oder hoch in der Luft. Es war augenscheinlich ein guter Start, einfach das Modell ausgestellt zu haben. (...) Mein Modell schwebte wie eine fliegende Untertasse aus Stahlbeton voller Löcher und Öffnungen zum Durchschauen, die Leute steckten ihre Köpfe hinein und wurden nicht schlau daraus.«[47] Nach der Eröffnung besucht Kiesler P.J.Clarkes Bar mit einigen Freunden, darunter die Reiss', Peggy Jackson, Luba Harrington, Sidney Janis, Leo Castelli sowie Bob Rauschenberg und Jasper Johns, »die von der Genauigkeit meiner kurvilinearen Tuschentwürfe der Wiener Originalpläne (1924) für das *Endless* beeindruckt waren«.[48]

43 Ibid., p. 269
43 Ebd., S. 269

44 Ibid., p. 281
44 Ebd., S. 281

45 Ibid., p. 282
45 Ebd., S. 282

46 Now in the Whitney Museum of American Art.
46 Jetzt im Whitney Museum of American Art.
47 Frederick Kiesler, *Inside the Endless House*, S. 299. Also Huxtable refers on the installation of the *Endless House*: »With the help of life-size photographs, the spectator can enter Frederick Kiesler's world of ›endless space‹, a kind of free-form Fun House, or gelatinous Cabinet of Dr. Caligari«, in: »The Architect as a Prophet«, publication unknown

47 Frederick Kiesler, *Inside the Endless House*, S. 299. A. L. Huxtable in Bezug auf die Installation des *Endless House*: »Mithilfe lebensgroßer Fotografien kann der Betrachter Friedrich Kieslers Welt des ›endlosen Raums‹ betreten, eine Art frei geformtes Fun House oder gallertiges Kabinett des Dr. Caligari«, in: »The Architect as a Prophet«, Publikationen unbekannt
48 Frederick Kiesler, *Inside the Endless House*, p. 300–302
48 Ebd., S. 300–302

October 2, 1960
Emily Genauer writes in the *Herald Tribune*: »A subtitle for *Visionary Architecture* (…) could have been ›A World They Never Made – Thank God‹. (…) Man is reduced to a robot, a drone, an animal. He is visualized as living in an endless cave, or on a series of saucers placed on the sea as if it were a table setting, or in a metropolis entirely covered by a great dome forever coming between him and the sky.«[49]

October 3, 1960
A journalist writes in *Newsweek*: »(…) a pumpernickel-shaped, highly sculptural *Endless House* (…). Kiesler claims that he will finally sees his house built by a venturesome family in Connecticut early next year (…) it will cost $ 80.000.«[50]

November 7, 1960
Kiesler writes »Hazard and the Endless House«.[51]

January 10 – 28, 1961
Exhibition of *Shell Sculptures and Galaxies* at Leo Castelli's.

March 30, 1961
Kiesler writes a letter to Mary Sisler offering to design and build the *Endless House* for $ 200.000 plus his own provisions.[52]

April 1, 1961
Kiesler reports in his journal: »A Florida Lady appeared at the last hour of the last Saturday afternoon of my show. A newcomer of the gallery, she called for Mr. Castelli and said, ›What's that?‹ Her finger pointed to what seemed a shell sculpture in concrete. Castelli answered, ›It is a model for the *Endless House*, a small version‹. ›An *Endless House*? Endless … I would love to live in it.‹«[53]

May 13, 1961
Kiesler is in Palm Beach to meet Mary Sisler and to discuss the possibility of building the *Endless House* on her estate.

May 23, 1961
Frederick Kiesler, Lillian Olinsey and Piero Dorazio meet in Kiesler's apartment to talk about the *Endless House*. Kiesler records Dorazio's comments in his journal: »Last year I saw the model of the *Endless House*. It is the most complete object I have ever seen, representing or containing, or whatever you want to say, the visions of art – of sculpture, of architecture – and of its philosophy. It is a piece of poetry in a way, it really is something that I can't describe here, something so complete and full of diversities, like an Encyclopedia Britannica of Art.«[54]

---

2. Oktober 1960
Emily Genauer schreibt in der *Herald Tribune*: »Ein Untertitel für *Visionary Architecture* (…) könnte auch gelautet haben: ›Eine Welt, die sie nie schufen – Gott sei Dank‹. (…) Der Mensch ist reduziert auf einen Roboter, eine Drohne, ein Tier. Man sieht ihn in einer endlosen Höhle leben oder in mehreren Untertassen, die auf dem Meer schwimmen wie auf einem gedeckten Tisch, oder in einer Metropolis, über der sich eine gewaltige Kuppel wölbt, die ihn für immer vom Himmel trennt.«[49]

3. Oktober 1960
Ein Journalist schreibt in *Newsweek*: »(…) ein pumpernickelförmiges, höchst skulpturales *Endless House*. (…) Laut Kiesler ist es endlich so weit, Anfang nächsten Jahres wird sein Haus von einer wagemutigen Familie in Connecticut gebaut werden. (…) Die Kosten: 80.000 $.«[50]

7. November 1960
Kiesler schreibt »Hazard and the Endless House«.[51]

10. – 28. Januar 1961
Die Leo Castelli Gallery zeigt *Shell Sculptures and Galaxies*.

30. März 1961
Kiesler schreibt einen Brief an Mary Sisler mit dem Angebot, das *Endless House* für 200.000 $ plus Provision zu entwerfen und zu bauen.[52]

1. April 1961
Kiesler berichtet in seinem Tagebuch: »Eine Lady aus Florida kam am letzten Samstagnachmittag meiner Show kurz vor Schluss in die Galerie. Es war ihr erster Besuch, sie fragte nach Mr. Castelli und erkundigte sich: ›Was ist das?‹ Ihr Finger deutete auf eine Schalenskulptur aus Beton. Castelli antwortete: ›Das ist ein Modell des *Endless House*, eine kleine Version.‹ ›Ein *Endless House*? Endlos … darin würde ich gerne wohnen.‹«[53]

13. Mai 1961
Kiesler ist in Palm Beach, um Mary Sisler zu treffen und über Möglichkeiten zu sprechen, das *Endless House* auf ihrem Anwesen zu errichten.

23. Mai 1961
Friedrich Kiesler, Lillian Olinsey und Piero Dorazio treffen sich in Kieslers Wohnung zu Gesprächen über das *Endless House*. Kiesler hält Dorazios Kommentare in seinem Tagebuch fest: »Vergangenes Jahr sah ich das Modell des *Endless House*. Es ist das vollkommenste Objekt, das ich je gesehen habe, es verkörpert oder enthält, oder wie immer man es nennen will, die Visionen der Kunst – der Bildhauerei, der Architektur – und ihrer Philosophie. Es ist auf eine Weise ein Stück Poesie, es ist wirklich etwas, das ich hier nicht beschreiben kann, etwas so Vollkommenes und Facettenreiches wie eine Encyclopedia Britannica der Kunst.«[54]

---

49 »Museum Shows Architect's Dream World«, in: *New York Herald Tribune*, October 2, 1960. A photograph of the *Endless House* represents the exhibition in most of the articles published on the show at the MoMA.
49 »Museum Shows Architect's Dream World«, in: *New York Herald Tribune*, 2. Oktober 1960. Eine Fotografie des *Endless House* repräsentiert die Ausstellung in den meisten anlässlich der Schau im MoMA erscheinenden Artikeln.

50 »Dreamy Stuff to Live In«, in: *Newsweek*, October 3, 1960
50 »Dreamy Stuff to Live In«, in: *Newsweek*, 3. Oktober 1960
51 In: *Art News*, November 7, 1960
51 In: *Art News*, 7. November 1960

52 Letter from Frederick Kiesler to Mary Sisler, typescript
52 Brief Friedrich Kieslers an Mary Sisler, Typoskript

53 F. Kiesler, *Inside the Endless House*, p. 417
53 F. Kiesler, *Inside the Endless House*, S. 417

54 Ibid., p. 412
54 Ebd., S. 412
55 Letter from Frederick Kiesler to Mary Sisler, typescript. Mary Sisler answers some days later: »Since the design of the *Endless House* I reviewed with you in New York is not going to be the house you propose to build now I cannot see how any suggestion on my part could be of any help to you. I would have to have some ideas as to the design, shape or style that you have in mind before I could even think about it.«
55 Brief Friedrich Kieslers an Mary Sisler, Typoskript. Mary Sisler antwortet einige Tage später: »Da das Modell des *Endless House*, das ich mit Ihnen in New York besprochen habe, nichts mit dem Haus zu tun haben wird, das Sie mir nun vorschlagen, sehe ich nicht, wie Ihnen irgendeine Anregung meinerseits dienlich sein könnte. Ich müsste eine Ahnung vom Entwurf, Äußeren oder Stil haben, die Ihnen vorschweben, bevor ich überhaupt darüber nachdenken kann.«

June 21, 1961
Kiesler writes to Mary Sisler informing her about the design of her *Endless House* in Florida: »The design which finally will emerge will not be a copy of the house which is known, but your house will be particularly planned and designed for your area and for your personal needs. It has to be tailored from these points of view and demands therefore careful preparation before design conclusions are fixed. I would very much appreciate it if you would inform me of any suggestion, additions or omissions that you would like to have me know.«[55] The project is not realized, since Mary Sisler admitted to being interested in building the *Endless House* as »a magnet for property buyers« and not as a house for herself.[56]

July 1961
Thomas H. Creighton interviews Frederick Kiesler in *Progressive Architecture*.[57]

October 1961
Some letters to the Editor in *Progressive Architecture* follow the long interview in which Kiesler expounds his ideas: »Dear Editor: I took great delight in your article on Kiesler. A man so full of wonder, capacity to think, and desire to invent is the maker of other men. Through his work he teaches. Louis I. Kahn, Philadelphia, Pa.« and: »Dear Editor: I have kept myself with considerable effort from crying out loud about your New Sensualism, New Chaoticism, and I shall hold on to myself even now that you have discovered the past of Friedrich Kiesler. You must have been the last man alive who had not heard about it (...). Sybil Moholy-Nagy, New Milford, Conn.«[58]

April 1963
A photograph of the *Endless House* is published in an article as exemplary for conical shell construction. The *Endless House* uses »a roof-orien-ted structural form as a vertical structural element«.[59]

August 1, 1963
Kiesler writes to Dorazio for information about the Venice Biennale where he sought to promote the *Endless House*.[60]

November 1964
Michel Ragon writes an article where he indicates that Kiesler is the pioneer of a curved feminine architecture, seen as a reaction to the functionalist right angles and boxes.[61]

21. Juni 1961
Kiesler schreibt an Mary Sisler, den Entstehungsprozess ihres *Endless House* in Florida betreffend: »Der Entwurf, der sich schließlich herauskristallieren wird, wird keine Kopie des Hauses sein, wie man es kennt, sondern Ihr Haus wird speziell geplant und auf Ihr Umfeld und Ihre persönlichen Bedürfnisse abgestimmt sein. Es muss von diesen Gesichtspunkten her maßgeschneidert werden und erfordert deshalb sorgfältige Vorbereitung, bevor die endgültige Konstruktion feststeht. Ich wäre äußerst dankbar für Anregungen, Erweiterungen oder Unterlassungen, von denen Sie mich in Kenntnis setzen möchten.«[55] Das Projekt wird nicht realisiert, da Mary Sisler zugibt, das *Endless House* als »Attraktion für Grundstückskäufer« bauen zu wollen und nicht als Haus für sie selbst.[56]

Juli 1961
Thomas H. Creighton interviewt Friedrich Kiesler in *Progressive Architecture*.[57]

Oktober 1961
Leserbriefreaktionen in *Progressive Architecture* auf das ausführliche Interview, in dem Kiesler seine Ideen erläuterte: »Sehr geehrter Herausgeber, Ihr Artikel über Kiesler hat mir große Freude bereitet. Ein Mann, der derart voller Wunder, Denkfähigkeit und dem Wunsch zu erfinden steckt, prägt andere Menschen. Er lehrt durch seine Arbeit. Louis I. Kahn, Philadelphia, Pa.« und: »Sehr geehrter Herausgeber, ich musste mich sehr anstrengen, über Ihren Neuen Sensualismus und Neuen Chaotizismus nicht laut loszubrüllen, und ich werde mich auch jetzt beherrschen, wo Sie die Vergangenheit Friedrich Kieslers entdeckt haben. Sie müssen der letzte Mensch auf der Welt gewesen sein, der noch nichts davon gehört hatte (...). Sybil Moholy-Nagy, New Milford, Conn.«[58]

1. August 1963
Kiesler schreibt an Dorazio um Informationen über die Biennale in Venedig, auf der er für das *Endless House* werben will.[59]

April 1963
In einem Artikel erscheint eine Fotografie des *Endless House* als Beispiel einer konischen Schalenkonstruktion. Das *Endless House* verwende »eine dachorientierte Bauform als vertikales Strukturelement«.[60]

November 1964
Michel Ragon bezeichnet in einem Artikel Kiesler als Pionier einer kurvigen weiblichen Architektur, einer Reaktion auf funktionalistische rechte Winkel und Boxen.[61]

56 Ibid., p. 444
56 Ebd., S. 444

57 Thomas H. Creighton, »Kiesler's Pursuit of an Idea« (interview with F. Kiesler), in: *Progressive Architecture*, July 1961
57 Thomas H. Creighton, »Kiesler's Pursuit of an Idea« (Interview mit F. Kiesler), in: *Progressive Architecture*, Juli 1961
58 »Re: Kiesler: Additional Comments«, in: *Progressive Architecture*, October 1961
58 »Re: Kiesler: Additional Comments«, in: *Progressive Architecture*, Oktober 1961

59 »Could you be kind enough and tell me who is now the higher board of the Venice Biennale? These [Apollonio, Santomaso and Scarpa] were the three who were interested in building the model of the *Endless House* in Venice – the money to be found in the US.« Letter from Frederick Kiesler to Piero Dorazio, Gift of Piero Dorazio
59 »Könnten Sie bitte so freundlich sein, mir zu sagen, wer nun im Komitee der Biennale von Venedig sitzt? Diese drei [Apollonio, Santomaso und Scarpa] zeigten Interesse, das Modell des *Endless House* in Venedig zu bauen – wenn das Geld aus den Staaten kommt.« Brief Friedrich Kieslers an Piero Dorazio, Typoskript; gestiftet von Piero Dorazio

60 »Endless House«, in: *Architectural and Engineering News*, April 1963, vol. 5, no. 4
60 »Endless House«, in: *Architectural and Engineering News*, April 1963, Bd. 5, No. 4

61 M. Ragon, »Le précurseur annonce l'architecture féminine des courbes«, in: *La Galerie des Arts*, November 1964
61 M. Ragon, »Le précurseur annonce l'architecture féminine des courbes«, in: *La Galerie des Arts*, November 1964

July 25, 1965
Reid B. Johnson writes to
Kiesler proposing to build the
Endless House as a museum of
contemporary art in Cleveland: »I can see an *Endless
House* dedicated to this purpose. It would be both a museum of contemporary art and a
teaching link between art and
science. (...) I think that your
work, and the continuous-ten-
sion *Endless* in particular,
has shown a great subjective
interlocking of technology and
pure aesthetics. You can see
why I am so eager for an adaptation of the 1959 *Endless* to
house this activity – the *Endless*
is a symbol of it in itself.«[62]

May/June 1966
Kiesler's text »The Future:
Notes on Architecture as
Sculpture« is published
posthomously in *Art in
America*.[63]

1966
A selection of Frederick
Kiesler's journals is published
under the title of *Inside the
Endless House. Art, People and
Architecture. A Journal*. In his
journals from 1956 to 1965,
Kiesler collects thoughts
about his life and his intellectual activity, focussing on the
difficulties and the joy of living
together with the utopia of the
Endless House.

→ see picture 84
→ Siehe Abb. 84

84

25. Juli 1965
Reid B. Johnson schreibt an
Kiesler mit dem Vorschlag,
das *Endless House* als Museum
moderner Kunst in Cleveland
zu bauen: »Ich sehe ein
diesem Zweck gewidmetes
Endless House vor mir. Es wäre
Museum moderner Kunst und
lehrendes Bindeglied zwischen
Kunst und Wissenschaft zugleich. (...) Ich glaube, dass Ihre
Arbeit, und das *Endless* mit
seiner kontinuierlichen Spannung im Besonderen, eine
großartige subjektive Verzah-
nung von Technologie und pu-
rer Ästhetik darstellt. Sie verstehen, warum ich so darauf
dränge, dass eine Adaptation
des *Endless* von 1959 diese
Aktivität beherbergt – das
Endless ist ein Symbol in sich
selbst.«[62]

Mai/Juni 1966
Kieslers Text »The Future:
Notes on Architecture as
Sculpture« wird posthum in
Art in America veröffentlicht.[63]

1966
Eine Auswahl aus Friedrich
Kieslers Tagebüchern
erscheint unter dem Titel
*Inside the Endless House. Art,
People and Architecture. A
Journal*. In seinen Tagebüchern von 1956 bis 1965 sam-
melte Kiesler Gedanken zu
seinem Leben und seiner
intellektuellen Tätigkeit mit
dem Schwerpunkt auf den
Freuden und Leiden einer
Existenz rund um die Utopie
des *Endless House*.

62 Letter from Reid B. Johnson to Frederick Kiesler, typescript. The letter
includes a *Prospectus for a Museum of
Contemporary Art in Cleveland*.
62 Brief Reid B. Johnsons an Friedrich
Kiesler, Typoskript. Dem Brief beigelegt
ist ein *Prospectus for a Museum of Contemporary Art in Cleveland*.

63 In: *Art in America*, May/June 1966
63 In: *Art in America*, Mai/Juni 1966

PLANÈTE magazine

Kiesler: je rêve d'une architecture féminine

En architecture, 1965 est une année Kiesler. Frédéric Kiesler publie en effet le livre de sa vie: *Journal d'un architecte* ou *la Recherche sans fin*. Le musée Guggenheim a consacré une exposition à ses sculptures, et le bâtiment que l'État d'Israël lui a commandé pour les manuscrits de la mer Morte est en voie d'achèvement.

« *La maison sans fin* », de Frédérick Kiesler.
(Photo Usis).

ratoire pour la recherche du dessin corréaliste » à l'université de Columbia, basant tous ses plans architectoniques et plastiques sur la structure du noyau cellulaire et cela bien avant la vogue des théories atomiques. En 1942, Peggy Guggenheim l'engageait pour aménager sa galerie *l'Art du siècle*. Il a expliqué, en 1947, dans son *Manifeste du corréalisme,* comment il avait conçu alors l'idée d'un musée dont les tableaux seraient débarrassés de leur cadre et ce cadre remplacé par « l'architecture générale de la pièce. Le tableau faisait partie de l'ensemble architectural et n'en était plus artificiellement isolé... Pour séparer les tableaux de l'arrière-plan sans interrompre la continuité des relations qui les unissaient, je pris le mur rigide et droit et je le recourbai. Un support, sorte de bras en bois de plusieurs pieds de long, était incorporé dans la concavité du mur et supportait le tableau. Le tableau semble flotter librement. C'est un monde en soi que le peintre a conçu et que l'architecte a mis à l'ancre. »

TOUT COMMENCE

On reconnaît là le principe même d'accrochage des tableaux de l'actuel musée Guggenheim, construit par Wright à New York en 1959. Et cette innovation est en général attribuée à Wright et non à Kiesler. De même l'aérogare de la T.W.A. à New York Kennedy, par Saarinen, paraît beaucoup moins nouvelle lorsqu'on connaît les dessins de la maison sans fin de Kiesler et les murs courbes de la « World House Gallery » que Kiesler a construite à New York.
— Jusqu'à présent, me disait Kiesler l'hiver dernier, l'architecture était masculine. Maintenant commence une architecture féminine, avec une continuité sans fin, comme le corps féminin.

Michel Ragon.

scénographique. C'est à ce titre de théoricien d'une scénographie nouvelle que Frédérick J. Kiesler était appelé à New York en 1926, et construisait deux ans plus tard, dans cette ville, un cinéma à quatre écrans.
Kiesler n'est plus reparti des États-Unis, sinon pour des voyages provisoires. En 1936, il fondait un « Labo-

185

Architecture

FREDERICK KIESLER 1890–1965
FRIEDRICH KIESLER 1890–1965

1890   Frederick J. Kiesler was born to Julius Kiesler and Maria Meister on September 22 in Cernauti, Romania.

1908–09   First record of Kiesler in Vienna at the K. K. Wiener Technische Hochschule.

1910   Enters Akademie der Bildenden Künste, Vienna which he leaves without a degree.

1914–17   According to his own account, he serves in the Austrian military press corps.

1920   On August 19, Kiesler marries the philology student Steffi Frischer in the Vienna Synagogue. In his own account, he works with Adolf Loos on a slum-clearing project.

1921   Travels to Berlin, where he remains for three months.

1923   Kiesler works on his first set design for Karel Čapek's play *R.U.R.* which premieres in Berlin.

1924   He organises and designs the *Internationale Ausstellung neuer Theatertechnik* in Vienna. For this exhibition he develops the revolutionary concept of the *Space Stage* and his radical *L+T* installation system.

1925   Josef Hoffmann invites him to design and organize a theater display for the Austrian theater section at the *Exposition Internationale des Arts Décoratifs et Industriels Modernes* in Paris. Kiesler builds the *City in Space* as an architectural vision of a floating city. In the same year he works on architectural plans for a horizontal skyscraper, and for a theater called *Universal. Endless Without a Stage*.

1926   Jane Heap, editor of *The Little Review*, invites Kiesler to direct the *International Theater Exposition* in New York. Frederick and Steffi Kiesler set sail for New York with more than forty crates of exhibits. The Kieslers then settle in New York.

1927   The Kieslers collaborate with Katherine Dreier for an exhibition at the Anderson Gallery. Steffi is employed at the New York Public Library where she workes until 1959.

1928   Kiesler begins to design store windows for *Saks Fifth Avenue* and becomes member of the *AUDAC* (American Union of Decorative Artists and Craftsmen).

1929   Kiesler builds the *Film Guild Cinema* in New York.

1930   He obtains the architect's licence from the New York State and establishes the *Planners Institute*. His book *Contemporary Art Applied to the Store and its Display* is published by Brentano. In this year he goes to Paris during the summer.

1931   Kiesler wins the competition for the *Woodstock Theater*, however, the project was never built. Frank Lloyd Wright is also one of the participants in this architectural competition.

1933   Kiesler builds a full-scale model of the *Space House* in the show room of a New York furniture company. Begins to work as stage designer for the Juilliard School of Music.

1934   Storefront design for *Jay's Shoes*. He works on a theater production *Helen Retires*.

1935   Designs various pieces of furniture for the apartment of Alma Mergentine. Renovates the interior of *Westermann Bookstore* in New York City.

1936   Submits patents for a *Party Lounge & Furniture Construction* and *Lamp & Table Construction*. Begins to write his book titled *Magic Architecture*.

1937   Appointed professor at the School of Architecture at Columbia University where he establishes the *Laboratory for Design Correlation*. Starts working on the *Vision Machine*.

1938   *Sleeping Beauty* opens at the Juilliard School of Music. Kiesler works with his students on the *Mobile Home Library*, the first product of the *Laboratory for Design Correlation*.

1939   Publishes »On Correalism and Biotechnique« in *Architectural Record*.

1940   Lectures at Ann Arbor Design Conference and at Yale University and works on two theater productions: *Le Donne Curiose* and *Magic Flute*.

1890   Friedrich Kiesler wird am 22. September in Czernowitz, Rumänien als Sohn von Julius Kiesler und Maria Meister geboren.

1908–09   Kiesler ist erstmals in Wien als Student an der Wiener Technischen Hochschule dokumentarisch erfasst.

1910   Er inskribiert an der Akademie der Bildenden Künste in Wien. Ohne Abschlusszeugnis tritt er drei Jahre später aus.

1914–17   Kiesler dient – nach eigenen Angaben – im österreichischen Kriegspressedienst.

1920   Am 19. August heiratet er in der K.k. Wiener Synagoge die Philologie-Studentin Steffi Frischer. Berichte über eine Mitarbeit bei Adolf Loos für ein Siedlungsprojekt der Nachkriegszeit sind nicht nachweisbar.

1921   Kiesler hält sich im Herbst drei Monate in Berlin auf.

1923   Kiesler entwirft sein erstes Bühnenbild für Karel Čapeks Theaterstück *W.U.R.* in Berlin.

1924   Kiesler organisiert und gestaltet im Wiener Konzerthaus die *Internationale Ausstellung neuer Theatertechnik*. Dafür konzipiert er die Raumbühne und das *L+T*-Ausstellungssystem.

1925   Josef Hoffmann beauftragt ihn, die Österreichische Theatersektion auf der Pariser *Exposition Internationale des Arts Décoratifs et Industriels Modernes* einzurichten. Kiesler entwirft die *Raumstadt* als Vision einer schwebenden Stadt der Zukunft. Im selben Jahr arbeitet er an Architekturentwürfen für einen horizontalen Wolkenkratzer und für ein Theater mit dem Titel *Universal. Endless Without a Stage*.

1926   Auf Einladung von Jane Heap, Herausgeberin von *Little Review*, bringen Friedrich und Steffi Kiesler mehr als vierzig Kisten mit Ausstellungsstücken für die *International Theater Exposition* im Steinway Building nach New York. Ab diesem Zeitpunkt leben die Kieslers in New York.

1927   Die Kieslers arbeiten zusammen mit Katherine Dreier an einer Ausstellung in der Anderson Gallery. Steffi beginnt an der New York Public Library zu arbeiten, wo sie bis 1959 bleibt.

1928   Kiesler gestaltet Schaufenster für das Warenhaus *Saks Fifth Avenue*. Er ist Mitglied der *AUDAC* (American Union of Decorative Artists and Craftsmen).

1929   Kiesler plant und baut das *Film Guild Cinema*.

1930   Er erhält die Architekturlizenz des Staates New York und gründet das Planungsbüro *Planners Institute*. Bei Brentano erscheint sein Buch *Contemporary Art Applied to the Store and its Display*. Im Sommer fährt Kiesler zusammen mit Steffi nach Paris, wo sie bis Oktober bleiben.

1931   Kiesler gewinnt gegen Frank Lloyd Wright den Wettbewerb für ein *Doppeltheater für Woodstock*. Es wird nicht realisiert.

1933   Kiesler entwirft das *Space House*, ein 1:1-Modell für ein Einfamilienhaus. Er beginnt als Bühnenbildner an der Juilliard School of Music.

1934   Kiesler beginnt sein Geschäftsdesign für *Jay's Shoes*. Kieslers erste Inszenierung – *Helen Retires* – hat an der Juilliard School of Music Premiere.

1935   Er arbeitet an Möbelentwürfen und erhält den Auftrag, die Wohnungseinrichtung für Alma Mergentine zu entwerfen. Er renoviert den *Westermann Bookstore* in New York.

1936   Kiesler reicht das Patent für eine *Party Lounge & Furniture Construction* sowie für eine *Lamp & Table Construction* ein. Er beginnt das Buch *Magic Architecture*.

1937   An der School of Architecture der Columbia University gründet er das *Laboratory for Design Correlation* und beginnt mit den Arbeiten an der *Vision Machine*.

1938   *Sleeping Beauty* feiert an der Juilliard School of Music mit Kieslers Bühnenbild und Kostümentwürfen Premiere. Kiesler arbeitet gemeinsam mit seinen Studenten an der *Mobile Home Library*, das erste Produkt des *Laboratory for Design Correlation*.

1939   Kiesler publiziert »On Correalism and Biotechnique: Definition and Test of a New Approach to Building Design« in *Architectural Record*.

1942   Invited by Peggy Guggenheim, Kiesler develops a new exhibition method for *Art of This Century* Gallery.
1943   Collaboration with the magazine *VVV*.
1944   Participates in *The Imagery of Chess* at the Julien Levy Gallery with John Cage, Alexander Calder, Max Ernst, Arshile Gorky, Roberto Matta.
1945   Prepares layout for André Breton's *Ode à Charles Fourier*, published in 1947.
1946   He designs a stage set for Jean Paul Sartre's *No Exit*
1947   Kiesler designs the Surrealist exhibition *Blood Flames* at the Hugo Gallery in New York and the installation for the *Exposition Internationale du Surréalisme* at the Maeght Gallery in Paris. He writes the »Manifeste du Corréalisme« published in June 1949 in *L'Architecture d'Aujourd'hui*.
1948   Kiesler works on a *Galaxial Portrait* of Wilfredo Lam and organizes the window display for *NEON* Magazine at Gotham Book Mart. Premier of *Le Pauvre Matelot*. For this stage design he creates a large wooden sculpture which he develops into his first sculptural *Galaxy*.
1950   The first model of the *Endless House* is included in the exhibition *The Muralist and the Modern Architect* at the Kootz Gallery.
1951   CBS elects Kiesler »Architect of the Year«. Starts to work on a wooden *Galaxy* for Philip Johnson's house at New Canaan. In June, The Museum of Modern Art acquires the small *Endless House* model and some related drawings.
1952   His *Galaxy* for *Le Pauvre Matelot* is included in Dorothy Miller's show *Fifteen Americans*.
1954   The Sidney Janis Gallery shows painted *Galaxies* in its first one-artist exhibition.
1955   Kiesler's *Galaxies* are shown in the Museum of Fine Arts in Houston. He designs a temporary theater for the Empire State Music Festival in Ellenville, New York. Spends the month of August in Vallauris, France working on a clay sculpture.
1956   Performs in Richter's movie *8 x 8* dressed as a Minotaur. Draws plans for an apartment house in Washington Square and for the Steifel Building for Paul Tishman, both not built.
1957   In collaboration with his partner Armand Bartos, Kiesler begins conceptual work on the *Shrine of the Book* in Jerusalem. The *World House Gallery*, a project by Kiesler and Bartos, opens in New York. He works on the reconstruction of a Moorish-Venetian theater at Caramoor in Katonah, New York.
1958   Receives a grant for the realization of preliminary sketches for an *Endless House* to be built in the garden of the Museum of Modern Art in New York. Starts working on the *Shell Sculptures*.
1959   Works with Armand Bartos on the design for the Ullman Research Center for Health and Science at the Yeshiva University in New York. The project was not realized.
1960   Receives a grant from the Ford Foundation for studies and a model of a *Universal Theater* for a competition on the theme *The Ideal Theater*. The Museum of Modern Art shows a large model of the *Endless House* in the exhibition *Visionary Architecture*.
1961   One-man show *Shell Sculptures* and *Galaxies* at the Leo Castelli Gallery. Negotiates with Mary Sisler for the construction of an *Endless House* in Palm Beach, Florida. Travels to Rome and Paris.
1962   Kiesler develops numerous sketches for a *Grotto for Meditation* for Jane Owen in New Harmony, Indiana.
1963   He begins the large environmental sculpture *Us-You-Me* and assembles journal notes and other writings for *Inside the Endless House*, a book of his recollections published posthumously in 1966 by Simon & Schuster. Steffi Kiesler dies September 3.
1964   On March 26, Kiesler marries Lillian Olinsey. Works on his sculpture *Bucephalus*.
1965   In April, Kiesler flies to Jerusalem for the opening ceremony of the *Shrine of The Book*. On December 27, Frederick Kiesler dies in New York.

1940   Er präsentiert an der Ann Arbor Design Conference eine Resolution über Design und hält Vorträge an der Yale University. Er stattet die Opernproduktionen *Le Donne Curiose* und *Zauberflöte* an der Juilliard School of Music aus.
1942   Auf Einladung von Peggy Guggenheim entwickelt Kiesler für die Gestaltung der Galerie *Art of This Century* radikal neue Präsentationsformen für Kunst.
1943   Kooperation mit der Zeitschrift *VVV*.
1944   Er nimmt in der Galerie Julien Levy an der Ausstellung *The Imagery of Chess* gemeinsam mit verschiedenen Künstlern teil. Unter ihnen John Cage, Alexander Calder, Max Ernst, Arshile Gorky und Roberto Matta.
1945   Er arbeitet am Layout zu André Bretons *Ode à Charles Fourier*.
1946   Er gestaltet das Bühnenbild für Jean Paul Sartres *No Exit*.
1947   Für die New Yorker Hugo Gallery gestaltet Kiesler die surrealistische Ausstellung *Blood Flames*, für die Pariser Galerie Maeght die *Exposition Internationale du Surréalisme*. Er verfasst das »Manifeste du Corréalisme«, das im Juni 1949 in *L'Architecture d'Aujourd'hui* veröffentlicht wird.
1948   Kiesler beendet die Arbeiten am *Galaxial Portrait* von Wilfredo Lam. Für das Magazin *NEON* gestaltet er eine Auslage im Gotham Book Mart. Für die Premiere von *Le Pauvre Matelot* an der Juilliard School of Music entwirft Kiesler eine hölzerne Konstruktion, aus der er in den folgenden Jahren seine erste skulpturale *Galaxy* entwickelt.
1950   In der Kootz Gallery wird das erste Modell für ein *Endless House* ausgestellt.
1951   CBS wählt Kiesler zum »Architect of the Year«. Er arbeitet an der *Galaxy* für Philip Johnsons Haus im New Canaan. Das Museum of Modern Art kauft das kleine Modell des *Endless House* sowie dazugehörende Zeichnungen.
1952   Seine *Galaxy* für *Le Pauvre Matelot* wird in Dorothy Millers Ausstellung *Fifteen Americans* gezeigt.
1954   Die Sidney Janis Galerie zeigt in einer ersten Einzelausstellung *Galaxien* von Kiesler.
1955   Kieslers *Galaxies* werden im Museum für Bildende Kunst in Houston gezeigt. Für das Empire State Music Festival in Ellenville, New York errichtet er ein Zelt als temporäres Theater. Im August verbringt er viel Zeit in Vallauris, Frankreich und arbeitet an Tonskulpturen, die heute verloren sind.
1956   Als Minotaurus verkleidet tritt Kiesler in Hans Richters Film *8 x 8* auf. Kiesler plant den Ausbau eines Hauses für John Jacob Astor in West Palm Beach, Florida, ein Apartment-Hochhaus für den Washington Square und das Steifel Building für Paul Tishman. Die Projekte werden nicht verwirklicht.
1957   Gemeinsam mit seinem Partner Armand Bartos beginnt Kiesler die Planungen für den *Shrine of the Book* in Jerusalem. Die von Kiesler und Bartos entworfene *World House Gallery* wird in New York eröffnet. Er rekonstruiert im venezianisch-maurischen Stil ein Theater in Caramoor, Katonah, NY.
1958   Er erhält ein Stipendium, um Vorentwurfpläne für das *Endless House* zu zeichnen, das im Garten des Museum of Modern Art errichtet werden soll. Er arbeitet an einer Reihe von Plastiken, die er *Shell Sculptures* nennt.
1959   Gemeinsam mit Armand Bartos arbeitet Kiesler an Entwürfen für das Ullman Research Center for Health and Science an der Yeshiva University, New York. Das Projekt wird nicht realisiert.
1960   Kiesler erhält von der Ford Foundation für den Wettbewerb *The Ideal Theater* ein Stipendium für Entwürfe und ein Modell des *Universal Theater* Das Museum of Modern Art lädt Kiesler zur Teilnahme an der Ausstellung *Visionary Architecture* ein.
1961   In der Leo Castelli Gallery findet Kieslers Einzelausstellung *Shell Sculptures und Galaxies* statt. Er verhandelt mit Mary Sisler über die Errichtung eines *Endless House* in West Palm Beach, Florida. Kiesler fährt nach Rom und Paris.
1962   Für Jane Owen erarbeitet Kiesler Pläne für die *Grotto for Meditation* in New Harmony, Indiana.
1963   Kiesler beginnt die Arbeiten an dem großen skulpturalen Environment *Us-You-Me*. Er stellt für eine Publikation Tagebuchaufzeichnungen und Erinnerungen zusammen, die 1966 posthum bei Simon & Schuster unter dem Titel *Inside the Endless House* erscheinen. Steffi Kiesler stirbt am 3. September.
1964   Am 26. März heiratet er Lillian Olinsey. Er arbeitet an der Skulptur *Bucephalus*.
1965   Im April fliegt Kiesler zur Eröffnung des *Shrine of the Book* nach Jerusalem. Am 27. Dezember stirbt Friedrich Kiesler in New York.

SELECTED BIBLIOGRAPHY
AUSGEWÄHLTE BIBLIOGRAFIE

Selected Bibliography on the *Endless House* /
Ausgewählte Bibliografie zu *Endless House*

– Frederick Kiesler, *Inside the Endless House*, Simon & Schuster,
New York 1966
– Dieter Bogner u.a. / a.o., *Friedrich Kiesler. Architekt Maler Bildhauer
1890–1965*, Wien 1988
– Yehuda Safran, *Frederick Kiesler (1890–1965)*, London 1989
– Lisa Phillips, *Frederick Kiesler*, New York 1989
– Maria Bottero, *Frederick Kiesler. Arte Architettura Ambiente*,
Milano 1996
– *Frederick Kiesler, Artiste – Architecte*, Paris 1996
– Siegfried Gohr, Gunda Luyken (Hrsg.), *Selected Writings*, Stuttgart 1996
– Dieter Bogner, *Friedrich Kiesler. Inside the Endless House*, Wien 1997
– Dieter Bogner, *Frederick Kiesler. En el interior del Endless House*,
Valencia 1997
– *Frederick J. Kiesler: Endless Space*, hrsg. von / edited by Dieter Bogner
u. a./a.o., Los Angeles 2001

Selected Clippings / Ausgewählte Zeitungsauschnitte

– Frederick Kiesler, »Notes on Architecture. The Space House:
Annotations at Random«, in: *Hound and Horn*, Januar/ März;
January/March 1934
– Frederick Kiesler, »Endless House – Space House«, in: *VVV no. 4*,
Februar / February 1944
– Frederick Kiesler, »Art and Architecture: Notes on the Spiral Theme
in Recent Architecture«, in: *Partisan Review*, Winter 1946
– Jean Arp, »L'œuf de Kiesler et la salle de superstition«, in: *Cahiers
d'Art*, XXII, 1947
– Frederick Kiesler, »Manifeste du Corréalisme«, in: *L' Architecture
d'Aujourd'hui*, Juni / June 1949
– Frederick Kiesler, »Pseudo-Functionalism in Modern Architecture«,
in: *Partisan Review*, Juli / July 1949
– *The Muralist and the Modern Architecture*, Kootz Gallery, New York,
Oktober / October 1950
– Aline B. Louchheim, »Architect, Painter – and the Mural«, in:
New York Times, 01.10.1950
– Doris Bryan, »Dealers Help Artists to Help Themselves«, in:
The Art Digest, 01.10.1950
– »Painters and Architects«, in: *Art News*, 06.10.1950
– »Architecture Plus«, in: *Quick*, 09.10.1950
– B. F. Dolbin, »Architektur und Bildende Kunst«, in: *Aufbau*, 13.10.1950
– Frederick Kiesler, »Frederick J. Kiesler's Endless House and Its
Psychological Lighting«, in: *Interiors*, November 1950
– »The Endless House: Frederick Kiesler, Architect«, in:
The Architectural Forum, November 1950
– Frederick Kiesler, »A Symposium on How to Combine Architecture,
Painting and Sculpture«, in: *Interiors*, 110/01, Mai / May 1951
– »Beyond the Horizon«, in: *Time*, 15.09.1952
– »Tough Prophet«, in: *Time*, 25.05.1959
– Thomas H. Creighton, »The New Sensualism I«, in: *Progressive
Architecture*, September 1959
– Thomas H. Creighton, »The New Sensualism II«, in: *Progressive
Architecture*, Oktober / October 1959
– »New Concepts of Architecture«, in: *Harper's Bazaar*,
Oktober / October 1959
– A. H. Podet, »Architect of the Endless House«, in: *Jerusalem Post*,
06.11.1959
– Arthur Drexler, »Frederick Kiesler and His Endless House«, in:
Vogue, Januar / January 1960

– Philip Johnson, »Three Architects«, in: *Art in America*, Frühling /
Spring 1960
– Ada Louise Huxtable, »Architecture on TV: Greatest Non-Building
Architect of Our Time Expounds His Ideas«, in: *New York Times*,
27.03.1960
– Frederick Kiesler, »Form is a Language«, in: *Art News*, April 1960
– Frederick Kiesler, »To the Art Editor/Building Architect«, in:
Sunday Times, 17.04.1960
– Emily Genauer, »Museum Shows Architect's Dream World«, in:
New York Herald Tribune, 02.10.1960
– »Dreamy Stuff to Live In«, in: *Newsweek*, 03.10.1960
– Frederick Kiesler, »Hazard and the Endless House«, in: *Art News*,
07.11.1960
– B. F. Dolbin, »Architektonische Reissbrett-Träume«, Publikation
unbekannt / publication unknown, Oktober / October 1960
– Ada Louise Huxtable, »The Architect as a Prophet«, Publikation
unbekannt / publication unknown, 1960
– John Canaday, »Art Dreamers at Work«, Publikation
unbekannt / publication unknown, 1960
– M. Ronnen, »Flights of Architectural Fancy«, Datum und Publikation
unbekannt / date and publication unknown (1960?)
– Frederick Kiesler, »Die Wunderstadt Brasilia«, in: *Aufbau*, 03.02.1961
– H. Borsick, »Fame is Endless«, in: *Plan Dealer*, 05.02.1961
– I. Rodríguez, »La casa sin fin«, in: *Arquitectura-Mexico*,
März / March 1961
– »Kiesler's Pursuit of an Idea« (Gespräch / Interview Thomas H.
Creighton mit / with F. Kiesler), in: *Progressive Architecture*,
Juli / July 1961
– »An Endless House in a Continuous Landscape«, in: *Progressive
Architecture*, September 1961
– »Re: Kiesler: Additional Comments«, in: *Progressive Architecture*,
Oktober / October 1961
– K. Fischer, »Utopien und Visionen des Bauens«, in: *Süddeutsche
Zeitung*, 02.10.1961
– J. Buschkiel, »Phantastische Architektur«, in: *Frankfurter Rundschau*,
04.10.1961
– »Det endeløse hus er formet«, in: *Berlingske Tidende*, 20.10.1961
– »Endless House«, in: *Architectural and Engineering News*, April 1963
– Michel Ragon, »Le précurseur annonce l'architecture féminine des
courbes«, in: *La Galerie des Arts*, November 1964
– Michel Ragon, »Je rêve d'une architecture féminine«, in:
Planète, No. 22, 1965
– Frederick Kiesler, »The Future: Notes on Architecture as Sculpture«,
in: *Art in America*, Mai / Juni; May / June 1966
– »All About Decorating/The Sculptured House«, in: *American Home*,
April 1969
– Cynthia Goodman, »The Current of Contemporary History: Frederick
Kiesler's Endless Research«, in: *Arts*, September 1979
– Antje von Graevenitz, »Oneindigheid en reductie. Frederick Kiesler's
Endless House«, in: *Archis*, II, November 1996
– Beatriz Colomina, »De psyche van het bouwen. Frederick Kiesler's
Space House«, in: *Archis*, II, November 1996
– Dieter Bogner u.a. / a.o., »Frederick Kiesler«, in: *Witte de With Cahier*,
Düsseldorf 1997
– Dieter Bogner, »En el interior de la Endless House«, in:
Quaderns d'arquitectura i urbanisme, No. 222, 2000
– Ben Van Berkel, Caroline Bos, »Una capacidad para lo interminable«,
in: *Quaderns d'arquitectura i urbanisme*, No. 222, 2000

INDEX OF ILLUSTRATIONS
ABBILDUNGSVERZEICHNIS

#		Size	Material	Inv. No.
1	Friedrich Kiesler bei der Arbeit am Modell des *Endless House* Frederick Kiesler with *Endless House* model in progress	9 cm x 13 cm 9 cm x 13 cm	Abzug vom Originalnegativ, Blaupause auf Fotopapier original negative print, blueprint on photographic paper	PHO 812 / 0 _ D43
2	*Magic Architecture*, 40er Jahre *Magic Architecture*, 1940s	28 cm x 21 cm (eine Seite) 28 cm x 21 cm (one page)	Papier auf Karton paper mounted on cardboard	TXT 606 / 0
3	Einblick in die Ausstellung Friedrich Kiesler: Endless House, MMK – Museum für Moderne Kunst Frankfurt am Main, 2003 (Foto Axel Schneider / MMK) View of the exhibition Frederick Kiesler: Endless House, MMK – Museum für Moderne Kunst Frankfurt am Main, 2003 (photo Axel Schneider / MMK)			
4	Kiesler mit dem Modell des *Endless House* Kiesler with the *Endless House* model	Vintage Print, s/w foto vintage print, b/w photo	20.5 cm x 25.3 cm, Foto: Hans Namuth 20.5 cm x 25.3 cm, photo Hans Namuth	801 / 0 801 / 0
5	*Magic Architecture*, 40er-Jahre, Umschlag *Magic Architecture*, 1940s, cover	31 cm x 23 cm 31 cm x 23 cm	Karton cardboard	TXT 606 / 0 TXT 606 / 0
6	*Magic Architecture*, 40er-Jahre *Magic Architecture*, 1940s	28 cm x 21 cm 28 cm x 21 cm	Papier auf Karton paper mounted on cardboard	TXT 606 / 0 TXT 606 / 0
7	*Magic Architecture*, 40er-Jahre *Magic Architecture*, 1940s	28 cm x 21 cm 28 cm x 21 cm	Papier auf Karton paper mounted on cardboard	TXT 606 / 0 TXT 606 / 0
8	*Magic Architecture*, 40er-Jahre *Magic Architecture*, 1940s	28 cm x 21 cm 28 cm x 21 cm	Papier auf Karton paper mounted on cardboard	TXT 606 / 0 TXT 606 / 0
9	*Magic Architecture*, 40er-Jahre *Magic Architecture*, 1940s	28 cm x 21 cm 28 cm x 21 cm	Papier auf Karton paper mounted on cardboard	TXT 606 / 0 TXT 606 / 0
10	*Magic Architecture*, 40er-Jahre *Magic Architecture*, 1940s	28 cm x 21 cm 28 cm x 21 cm	Recherchematerialien, Druck research materials, print	TXT 606 / 0 TXT 606 / 0
11	*Magic Architecture*, 40er-Jahre *Magic Architecture*, 1940s	28 cm x 21 cm 28 cm x 21 cm	Recherchematerialien, Druck research materials, print	TXT 606 / 0 TXT 606 / 0
12	*Magic Architecture*, 40er-Jahre *Magic Architecture*, 1940s	28 cm x 21 cm 28 cm x 21 cm	Recherchematerialien, Druck research materials, print	TXT 606 / 0 TXT 606 / 0
13	*Magic Architecture*, 40er-Jahre *Magic Architecture*, 1940s	28 cm x 21 cm (eine Seite) 28 cm x 21 cm (one page)	Papier auf Karton paper mounted on cardboard	TXT 606 / 0 TXT 606 / 0
14	*Magic Architecture*, 40er-Jahre *Magic Architecture*, 1940s	28 cm x 21 cm (eine Seite) 28 cm x 21 cm (one page)	Papier auf Karton paper mounted on cardboard	TXT 606 / 0 TXT 606 / 0
15	Architekturstudie (Studie zu *Paris Endless*), um 1950 Architectural study (Study for *Paris Endless*), around 1950	30.2 cm x 46 cm 30.2 cm x 46 cm	Gouache, Tempera auf Aquarellpapier gouache, tempera on watercolour paper	SFP 497 /0_LK 2307 SFP 497 /0_LK 2307
16	Studie zu *Maison en trois d'ètaches*, 1947 Study for *Maison en trois d'ètaches*, 1947	45.5 cm x 60.5 cm 45.5 cm x 60.5 cm	Zeichnung, Kugelschreiber auf Papier drawing, pen on paper	SFP 513 / 0 SFP 513 / 0
17	Architekturstudie (Studie zu *Paris Endless*), um 1950 Architectural study (Study for *Paris Endless*), around 1950	35 cm x 48.8 cm 30.2 cm x 46 cm,	Zeichnung, Kugelschreiber auf Papier, auf Karton montiert drawing, pen on paper glued on cardboard	SFP 509 / 0_LK 898 SFP 509 / 0_LK 898
18	Architekturstudie (Studie zu *Paris Endless*), um 1950 Architectural study, (Study for *Paris Endless*), around 1950	35.2 cm x 48.8 cm 35.2 cm x 48.8 cm	Zeichnung, Kugelschreiber auf Papier, auf Karton montiert collage, pen on paper glued on carton	SFP 515 /0_KE 4373 SFP 515 / 0_KE 4373
19	Architekturstudie (Studie zu *Paris Endless*), um 1950 Architectural study (Study for *Paris Endless*), around 1950	35 cm x 48.7 cm 35 cm x 48.7 cm	Zeichnung, Kugelschreiber auf Papier, auf Karton montiert drawing, pen on paper glued on cardboard	SFP 514 /0 _LK 896 SFP 514 /0_LK 896
20	Architekturstudie (Studie zu *Paris Endless*), um 1950 Architectural study (Study for *Paris Endless*), around 1950	35 cm x 48.8 cm 35 cm x 48.8 cm	Zeichnung, Kugelschreiber auf Papier, auf Karton montiert drawing, pen on paper glued on cardboard	SFP 487 /0 _ KE 4897 SFP 487 /0 _ KE 4897
21	Architekturstudie (Studie zu *Paris Endless*), um 1950 Architectural study (Study for *Paris Endless*), around 1950	35 cm x 48.7 cm 35 cm x 48.7 cm	Zeichnung, Kugelschreiber auf Papier, auf Karton montiert drawing, pen on paper glued on cardboard	SFP 508 / 0_LK 895 SFP 508 / 0_LK 895
22	Architekturstudie (Studie zu *Paris Endless*), um 1950 Architectural study (Study for *Paris Endless*), around 1950	43 cm x 63 cm 43 cm x 63 cm	Zeichnung, Kugelschreiber auf Papier, auf Karton montiert drawing, pen on paper glued on cardboard	SFP 507 / 0_KE 573 SFP 507 / 0_KE 573
23	*Chart of creation – mutation*, in: *Partisan Review*, Juli 1949 *Chart of creation – mutation*, in: *Partisan Review*, July 1949		Druck, Offset / Papier print on paper	
24	Architekturstudie (Studie zu *Paris Endless*), um 1950 Architectural study (Study for *Paris Endless*), around 1950	50 cm x 68.8 cm 50 cm x 68.8 cm	Collage, Tusche auf Papier, auf Karton montiert collage, ink on paper glued on cardboard	SFP 495 / 0 _ KE 569 SFP 495 / 0 _ KE 569
25	Studie für ein *Tooth House*, um 1950 Study for *Tooth House*, around 1950	21.4 cm x 27.7 cm 21.4 cm x 27.7 cm	Zeichnung, Kugelschreiber auf Papier drawing, pen on paper	SFP 529 /0 _ LK 219 SFP 529 /0 _ LK 219
26	Studie für ein *Tooth House*, um 1950 Study for *Tooth House*, around 1950	21.4 cm x 27.7 cm 21.4 cm x 27.7 cm	Zeichnung, Kugelschreiber auf Papier drawing, pen on paper	SFP 531 _ LK 206 SFP 531 _ LK 206
27	Studie für ein *Tooth House*, um 1950 Study for *Tooth House*, around 1950	21.5 cm x 28 cm 21.5 cm x 28 cm	Zeichnung, Kugelschreiber auf Papier drawing, pen on paper	SFP 522 / 0 _LK 220 SFP 522 / 0 _LK 220
28	Studie für ein *Tooth House*, um 1950 Study for *Tooth House*, around 1950	21.4 cm x 27.7 cm 21.4 cm x 27.7 cm	Zeichnung, Kugelschreiber auf Papier drawing, pen on paper	SFP 523 / 0 SFP 523 / 0

29	Studie für ein *Tooth House*, um 1950 Study for *Tooth House*, around 1950	21.5 cm x 28 cm 21.5 cm x 28 cm	Zeichnung, Kugelschreiber auf Papier drawing, pen on paper	SFP 521 /1 _ LK 216 b SFP 521/1 _ LK 216 b
30	Studie für ein *Tooth House*, um 1950 Study for *Tooth House*, around 1950	21.5 cm x 28 cm 21.5 cm x 28 cm	Zeichnung, Kugelschreiber auf Papier drawing, pen on paper	SFP 524 / 0 _ LK 224 SFP 524 / 0 _ LK 224
31	Studie für ein *Tooth House*, um 1950 Study for *Tooth House*, around 1950	21.5 cm x 28 cm 21.5 cm x 28 cm	Zeichnung, Kugelschreiber auf Papier drawing, pen on paper	SFP 524 / 1 _ LK 224 b SFP 524 / 1 _ LK 224 b
32	Studie für ein *Endless House*, um 1950 Study for *Endless House*, around 1950	13.7 cm x 21.3 cm 13.7 cm x 21.3 cm	Zeichnung, Kugelschreiber auf Papier drawing, pen on paper	SFP 578 / 0_ LK 198 SFP 578 / 0_ LK 198
33	Studie für ein *Endless House*, um 1950 Study for *Endless House*, around 1950	21.2 cm x 27.4 cm 21.2 cm x 27.4 cm	Zeichnung, Kugelschreiber auf Papier drawing, pen on paper	SFP 576 / 0 _ LK 5 SFP 576 / 0 _ LK 5
34	Studie für ein *Endless House*, um 1950 Study for *Endless House*, around 1950	13.7 cm x 21.3 cm 13.7 cm x 21.3 cm	Zeichnung, Kugelschreiber auf Papier drawing, pen on paper	SFP 577 / 0_LK 203 B SFP 577 / 0_LK 203 B
35	Studie für ein *Endless House*, um 1950 Study for *Endless House*, around 1950	14 cm x 21 cm 14 cm x 21 cm	Zeichnung, Kugelschreiber auf Papier drawing, pen on paper	SFP 689 / 0 SFP 689 / 0
36	*Endless-House*-Modell für die Kootz Gallery, 1950 *Endless House* Model for the Kootz Gallery, 1950	18.8 cm x 23.9 cm 18.8 cm x 23.9 cm	Abzug vom Originalnegativ, s/w Foto original negative print, b/w photo	PHO 618 / 0 PHO 618 / 0
37	*Endless-House*-Modell für die Kootz Gallery, 1950 *Endless House* Model for the Kootz Gallery, 1950	18.8 cm x 23.9 cm 18.8 cm x 23.9 cm	Abzug vom Originalnegativ, s / w Foto original negative print, b/w photo	PHO 619 / 0 PHO 619 / 0
38	*Endless-House*-Modell für die Kootz Gallery, 1950 *Endless House* Model for the Kootz Gallery, 1950	16.9 cm x 19.4 cm 16.9 cm x 19.4 cm	Abzug vom Originalnegativ, s / w Foto original negative print, b/w photo	PHO 631 / 0 PHO 631 / 0
39	Studie für ein *Endless House*, um 1950 Study for *Endless House*, around 1950	21.2 cm x 27.5 cm 21.2 cm x 27.5 cm	Zeichnung, Kugelschreiber auf Papier drawing, pen on paper	SFP 580 / 0 SFP 580 / 0
40	Modell für ein *Endless House*,1950 Model for *Endless House*, 1950	18 cm x 22.2 cm 18 cm x 22.2 cm	Abzug vom Originalnegativ, s/w Foto original negative print, b/w photo	PHO 622 / 0 PHO 622 / 0
41	Studie für ein *Endless House*, um 1950 Study for *Endless House*, around 1950	21.2 cm x 27.5 cm 21.2 cm x 27.5 cm	Zeichnung, Kugelschreiber auf Papier drawing, pen on paper	SFP 581 / 0 _KE 2201 SFP 581 / 0_KE 2201
42	Studie für ein *Endless House*, um 1950 Study for *Endless House*, around 1950	13.7 cm x 27.3 cm 13.7 cm x 27.3 cm	Zeichnung, Kugelschreiber auf Papier drawing, pen on paper	SFP 546 / 0 _ LK 87 SFP 546 / 0 _ LK 87
43	»*Endless House* and Its Psychological Lighting« in: *Interiors* »*Endless House* and Its Psychological Lighting« in: *Interiors*	35.7 cm x 25.3 cm 35.7 cm x 25.3 cm	Druck, Offset / Papier print on paper	CLP 437 / 0 CLP 437 / 0
44	Friedrich Kiesler mit Modell des *Endless House*, um 1960 Frederick Kiesler with model for *Endless House*, around 1960	20 cm x 25 cm 20 cm x 25 cm	Abzug vom Originalnegativ, s/w Foto, Foto: Irving Penn original negative print b/w photo, photo: Irving Penn	PHO 771 / 0 PHO 771 / 0
45	Friedrich Kiesler mit Modell des *Endless House* in Arbeit Frederick Kiesler with model for *Endless House* in progress	8.8 cm x 13.3 cm 8.8 cm x 13.3 cm	Abzug vom Originalnegativ, s/w Foto original negative print b/w photo	PHO 822 / 0 PHO 822 / 0
46	Modell des *Endless House*, um 1960 *Endless House* model, around 1960	20.5 cm x 23.3 cm 20.5 cm x 23.3 cm	Vintage Print, s/w Foto, Foto: G. Barrows vintage print, b/w photo, photo: G. Barrows	PHO 785 / 0 _ 18 PHO 785 / 0 _ 18
47	Modell des *Endless House*, um 1960 *Endless House* model, around 1960	20.5 cm x 23.3 cm 20.5 cm x 23.3 cm	Vintage Print, s /w Foto, Foto: G. Barrows vintage print, b/w photo, photo: G. Barrows	PHO 784 / 0 PHO 784 / 0
48	Studie zu *Endless House* (Beleuchtungssystem) Study for *Endless House* (lighting system)	12.7 cm x 20.3 cm 12.7 cm x 20.3 cm	Zeichnung, Bleistift auf Papier drawing, pencil on paper	SFP 667 _ 517 SFP 667 _ 517
49	Modell des *Endless House*, um 1960 *Endless House* model, around 1960	20.5 cm x 23.3 cm 20.5 cm x 23.3 cm	Vintage Print, s/w Foto, Foto: G. Barrows vintage print, b/w photo, photo: G. Barrows	PHO 786 / 0 _ 55 PHO 786 / 0 _ 55
50	Studie zu *Endless House* (Bett), 1958-1960 Study for *Endless House* (bed), 1958-1960	21 cm x 29.6 cm 21 cm x 29.6 cm	Zeichnung, Bleistift / Kugelschreiber auf Papier drawing, pencil and pen on paper	SFP 646 / 0 _ 260 SFP 646 / 0 _ 260
51	Studie zu *Endless House*, 1958-1960 Study for *Endless House*, 1958-1960	21 cm x 29.6 cm 21 cm x 29.6 cm	Zeichnung, Kugelschreiber auf Papier drawing, pen on paper	SFP 666 / 0 SFP 666 / 0
52	Produktion der Drahtstruktur zum *Endless-House*-Modell Wire structure for *Endless House* model in progress	18.6 cm x 24 cm 18.6 cm x 24 cm	Abzug vom Originalnegativ, s/w Foto original negative print, b/w photo	PHO 718 / 0 PHO 718 / 0
53	Produktion der Drahtstruktur zum *Endless-House*-Modell Wire structure for *Endless House* model in progress	20.4 cm x 25.3 cm 20.4 cm x 25.3 cm	Abzug vom Originalnegativ, s/w Foto original negative print b/w photo	PHO 912 / 0 PHO 912 / 0
54	Modell des *Endless House* in Arbeit, um 1960 *Endless House* model in progress, around 1960	20.4 cm x 25.3 cm 20.4 cm x 25.3 cm	Abzug vom Originalnegativ, s /w Foto original negative print, b / w photo	PHO 725 / 0 PHO 725 / 0
55	Studie zu *Endless House*, 1958-1960 Study for *Endless House*, 1958-1960	21 cm x 29.6 cm 21 cm x 29.6 cm	Zeichnung, Bleistift auf Papier drawing, pencil on paper	SFP 690 / 0 SFP 690 / 0
56	Modell des *Endless House* in Arbeit, um 1960 *Endless House* model in progress, around 1960	12 cm x 24.4 cm 12 cm x 24.4 cm	Abzug vom Originalnegativ, s/w Foto original negative print, b/w photo	PHO 776 / 0 PHO 776 / 0
57	Studie zu *Endless House*, 1958-1960 Study for *Endless House*, 1958-1960	21 cm x 29.6 cm 21 cm x 29.6 cm	Zeichnung, Bleistift auf Papier drawing, pencil on paper	SFP 665 / 0 SFP 665 / 0
58	Studie zu *Endless House*, 1958-1960 Study for *Endless House*, 1958-1960	21 cm x 29.6 cm 21 cm x 29.6 cm	Zeichnung, Bleistift auf Papier drawing, pencil on paper	SFP 688 / 0 SFP 688 / 0
59	*When I Conduct*, um 1960 *When I Conduct*, around 1960	28 cm x 22 cm (2 Seite) 28 cm x 22 cm (2 pages)	Typoskript, Schreibmaschine / Bleistift typescript, typewriter and pencil	TXT 608 / 0 TXT 608 / 0
60	Modell des *Endless House* (klein) in Arbeit, um 1960 *Endless House* model (small) in progress, around 1960	9 cm x 9 cm 9 cm x 9 cm	Vintage Print, s/w Foto vintage print, b/w photo	PHO 690 / 0 PHO 690 / 0
61	Modell des *Endless House* (klein) in Arbeit, um 1960 *Endless House* model (small) in progress, around 1960	9 cm x 9 cm 9 cm x 9 cm	Vintage Print, s/w Foto vintage print, b/w photo	PHO 692 / 0 PHO 692 / 0

62	Modell des *Endless House* (klein) in Arbeit, um 1960 *Endless House* model (small) in progress, around 1960	9 cm x 9 cm 9 cm x 9 cm	Vintage Print, s/w Foto vintage print, b/w photo	PHO 691 / 0 PHO 691 / 0
63	Modell des *Endless House* (klein) in Arbeit, um 1960 *Endless House* model (small) in progress, around 1960	8.8 cm x 13.3 cm 8.8 cm x 13.3 cm	Vintage Print, s/w Foto vintage print, b/w photo	PHO 674 / 0 _ D 43 PHO 674 / 0 _ D 43
64	Modell des *Endless House* (Schnitt) in Arbeit, , um 1960 *Endless House* Model (section) in progress, around 1960	9 cm x 9 cm 9 cm x 9 cm	Vintage Print, s/w Foto vintage print, b/w photo	PHO 665 / 0 PHO 665 / 0
65	Modell des *Endless House* (Schnitt) in Arbeit, um 1960 *Endless House* model (section) in progress, around 1960	9 cm x 9 cm 9 cm x 9 cm	Vintage Print, s/w Foto vintage print, b/w photo	PHO 658 / 0 PHO 658 / 0
66	Modell des *Endless House* (Schnitt) in Arbeit, um 1960 *Endless House* model (section) in progress, around 1960	9 cm x 9 cm 9 cm x 9 cm	Vintage Print, s/w Foto vintage print, b/w photo	PHO 669 / 0 PHO 669 / 0
67	Modell des *Endless House* (Schnitt) in Arbeit, um 1960 *Endless House* model (section) in progress, around 1960	9 cm x 9 cm 9 cm x 9 cm	Vintage Print, s/w Foto vintage print, b/w photo	PHO 660 / 0 PHO 660 / 0
68	Kieslers Interview für CBS, 1960 Kiesler´s interview on CBS, 1960	27´ 11˝ 27´ 11˝	Video VHS. Videostills video VHS, video stills	MED 271 / 0 MED 271 / 0
69	Modell des *Endless House*, um 1960 *Endless House* model, around 1960	21 cm x 25 cm, 21 cm x 25 cm,	Vintage Print, s/w Foto vintage print, b/w photo	PHO 913 / 0 PHO 913e / 0
70	Studie zum *Sisler House*, 1961 Study for *Sisler House*, 1961	48 cm x 60.5 cm 48 cm x 60.5 cm	Zeichnung, Bleistift auf Transparentpapier drawing, pencil on transparent paper	SFP 6420 _ KE 5094 SFP 6420 _ KE 5094
71	Studie zum *Sisler House*, 1961 Study for *Sisler House*, 1961	48 cm x 60.5 cm 48 cm x 60.5 cm	Zeichnung, Bleistift auf Transparentpapier drawing, pencil on transparent paper	SFP 642 / 0 SFP 642 / 0
72	Studie zum *Sisler House*, 1961 Study for *Sisler House*, 1961	47.6 cm x 59.8 cm 47.6 cm x 59.8 cm	Zeichnung, Bleistift auf Transparentpapier drawing, pencil on transparent paper	SFP 645 / 0 SFP 645 / 0
73	Studie zum *Sisler House*, 1961 Study for *Sisler House*, 1961	47.8 cm x 59.8 cm 47.8 cm x 59.8 cm	Zeichnung, Bleistift auf Transparentpapier drawing, pencil on transparent paper	SFP 636 / 0 _KE 5140 SFP 636 / 0 _KE 5140
74	Studie zum *Sisler House*, 1961 Study for *Sisler House*, 1961	35 cm x 40.6 cm 35 cm x 40.6 cm	Zeichnung, Bleistift auf Transparentpapier drawing, pencil on transparent paper	SFP 643 / 0 _KE 5117 SFP 643 / 0 _KE 5117
75	*Sisler House*, Gesamtplan mit Aufriss und Seitenriss, 1961 *Sisler House*, Plans and elevations, 1961	100 cm x 220 cm 100 cm x 220 cm	Blaupause auf Papier blueprint on paper	PLN 505 / 0 PLN 505 / 0
76	Kiesler und Hans Arp, um 1950 Kiesler and Hans Arp, around 1950	9.7 cm x 9.8 cm 9.7 cm x 9.8 cm	Abzug vom Originalnegativ, s/w Foto original negative print, b/w photo	PHO 817 / 0 PHO 817 / 0
77	*Partisan Review* Juli 1949, Umschlag *Partisan Review*, July 1949, cover	21 cm x 15 cm 21 cm x 15 cm	Offset / Papier printed paper	
78	Studie zur Raumgestaltung im *Salle des Superstitions*, 1947 Sketch for the *Salle des Superstitions*, 1947	21 cm x 25 cm 21 cm x 25 cm	Negativrepro, s/w Foto negative print, b/w photo	PHO 820 / 0 PHO 820 / 0
79	Kiesler in New York Tiergarten, 50er Jahre Kiesler at the New York Zoo, 1950s	13 cm x 18 cm 13 cm x 18 cm	Abzug vom Originalnegativ, s/w Foto original negative print, b/w photo	PHO 816 / 0 PHO 816 / 0
80	Kiesler bei der *Exposition internationale du Surréalisme*,1947 Kiesler at the *Exposition internationale du Surréalisme*, 1947	16 cm x 12 cm 16 cm x 12 cm	Vintage Print, s/w Foto, Foto: Denise Bellon vintage print, b/w photo, photo: Denise Bellon	PHO 821 / 0 PHO 821 / 0
81	Friedrich Kiesler vor einem Tempel, um 1958 Frederick Kiesler in front of a temple, around 1958	14 cm x 8.8 cm 14 cm x 8.8 cm	Abzug vom Originalnegativ, s/w Foto original negative print, b/w photo	PHO 810 / 0 PHO 810 / 0
82	»The Architect as a Prophet« in: *Time*, 25. Mai 1959 »The Architect as a Prophet« in: *Time*, May 25, 1959	43 cm x 14 cm 43 cm x 14 cm	Offset / Papier printed paper	CLP 438 / 0 CLP 438 / 0
83	Kiesler mit Leo Castelli und Salvatore Scarpitta, um 1960 Kiesler with Leo Castelli and Salvatore Scarpitta, around1960	8,8 cm x 13 cm 8.8 cm x 13 cm	Abzug vom Originalnegativ, s/w Foto original negative print, b/w photo	PHO 818 /0 PHO 818 / 0
84	M.Ragon, »Je réve d´une architecture féminine« in: *Planete* M. Ragon, »Je réve d´une architecture féminine« in: *Planete*	18 cm x 20 cm, 18 cm x 20 cm	Offset / Papier print on paper	CLP 440 / 0 CLP 440 / 0
85	Inside the *Endless House*, Umschlagfoto, 1966 Inside the *Endless House*, coverphoto, 1966	25 cm x 20 cm 25 cm x 20 cm	Abzug vom Originalnegativ, s/w Foto, Foto: Duane Michals original negative print, b/w photo, photo: Duane Michals	PHO 811 / 0 PHO 811 / 0

Österreichische Friedrich und Lillian Kiesler-Privatstiftung
Austrian Frederick and Lillian Kiesler Private Foundation

Stifter und Förderer Donors and Sponsors

Bundeskanzleramt Kunstsektion
Bundesministerium für Bildung, Wissenschaft und Kultur
Stadt Wien
Oesterreichische Nationalbank
Bank Austria Aktiengesellschaft
Österreichische Postsparkasse Aktiengesellschaft
Österreichische Lotterien Ges.m.b.H.
Wittmann Möbelwerkstätten Ges.m.b.H.
Wiener Städtische Allgemeine Versicherung Aktiengesellschaft
Bank für Arbeit und Wirtschaft Aktiengesellschaft
Hannes Pflaum
Dieter Bogner
Gertraud Bogner
John Sailer

Stiftungsvorstand Board

DieterBogner (Vorsitz)
Brigitte Böck
Thomas Drozda
Sylvia Eisenburger
Reinhold Hohengartner
Wolfgang Kos
Jason McCoy
Christa Winkler
Klaus Wölfer

Friedrich Kiesler-Zentrum, Wien Frederick Kiesler Center, Vienna

Krugerstraße 17/2, 1010 Wien, Österreich / Austria
Tel. 00 43/1/513 07 75
Fax 00 43/1/513 07 75-5
www.kiesler.org, foundation@kiesler.org

Direktion Director Monika Pessler
Sekretariat Secretary Catherine Dressler
Archiv Archive Harald Krejci
Forschung Research Valentina Sonzogni

Der Katalog wurde unterstützt durch die Förderer der
Österreichischen Friedrich und Lillian Kiesler-Privatstiftung
The catalogue was supported by the sponsors of
the Austrian Frederick and Lillian Kiesler Private Foundation

bm:bwk   KUNST   M   archive.it

Herausgeber Editor Österreichische Friedrich und Lillian Kiesler-Privatstiftung
MMK – Museum für Moderne Kunst Frankfurt am Main
Katalogkonzeption Concept of the catalogue Valentina Sonzogni, Harald Krejci
Übersetzungen Translations Petra Metelko, Verena Tomasik, Eva Stanzl
Lektorat Copy Editing Yasmin Kiss, Verena Tomasik, Simon Frearson
Grafische Gestaltung Graphic Design D+
Reproduktion Reproductions Österreichische Friedrich und Lillian Kiesler-Privatstiftung
CMB GmbH Digital Services, Wien
Gesamtherstellung Printed by Dr. Cantz'sche Druckerei, Ostfildern-Ruit

© 2003 für die abgebildeten Werke, falls nicht anders angegeben Österreichische Friedrich und Lillian Kiesler-Privatstiftung
© 2003 for the reproduced works if not otherwise indicated Austrian Frederick and Lillian Kiesler Private Foundation
© 2003 Hatje Cantz Publishers und Autoren / and authors

Erschienen bei Published by Hatje Cantz Verlag
Senefelderstraße 12
73760 Ostfildern-Ruit, Deutschland / Germany
Tel. 00 49/7 11/440 50
Fax 00 49/7 11/440 52 20
www.hatjecantz.de

Vertrieb in den USA Distribution in the US D.A.P., Distributed Art Publishers, Inc.
155 Avenue of the Americas, Second Floor
New York, N.Y., 10013-1507, USA
Tel. 001/212/627 19 99
Fax 001/212/627 94 84
ISBN 3-7757-1336-0

Dieses Buch erscheint anlässlich der Ausstellung Endless House (2003) im
This book was published on the occasion of the exhibition
Endless House (2003) at the
MMK – Museum für Moderne Kunst Frankfurt am Main
Domstraße 10
60311 Frankfurt am Main, Deutschland / Germany

Konzept Concept Udo Kittelmann (MMK), Dieter Bogner
Kuratoren Wien Curators Vienna Harald Krejci, Dieter Bogner
Kuratoren Frankfurt Curators Frankfurt Udo Kittelmann, Mario Kramer
Ausstellungsgestaltung Exhibition Design casino.container (Detlef Meyer-Voggenreiter, Uwe Wagner, Claudia Hoffmann)

Umschlagabbildung Cover Photo Kiesler vor dem Modell des Endless House, 92 cm x 35 cm, Vintage Print, Farbfoto
Kiesler before the Endless House model, 92 cm x 35 cm, vintage print, color photo
Foto: Hans Namuth

Mit freundlicher Unterstützung von With support from hessische
kultur
stiftung

»He was the kind of person you would expect to meet in a forest sitting on a mushroom«

Sidney Kingsley, eulogy for Frederick Kiesler, 1965, typoscript

»Er war ein Mensch, von dem man sich erwarten würde, ihn im Wald anzutreffen –
auf einem Pilz sitzend.«

Sidney Kingsley, Eloge auf Friedrich Kiesler, 1965, Typoskript